Barbara Riegel
&
Thomas Gillespie

Treat Your Ego in 4 Hours

Treat Your Ego in 4 Hours

"Brief Therapy":

The Complete Self-Help Program Hour by Hour

Thomas N. Rusk, M.D., and
Randolph A. Read, M.D.

PETER H. WYDEN / PUBLISHER NEW YORK

Designed by Paula Wiener
LIBRARY OF CONGRESS CATALOG CARD NUMBER: 74-14241
MANUFACTURED IN THE UNITED STATES OF AMERICA
ISBN: 0-88326-083-2

To our families

Acknowledgments

This being the first venture of book length by either author, we sought and received feedback and support from a variety of sources.

Alan Lakein served as matchmaker for us and Peter Wyden, our publisher.

Pat Palacios typed the manuscript, revision after revision, and, more importantly, she contributed creative suggestions throughout.

Our staff at Western Institute of Human Resources in San Diego has been involved concretely and spiritually from the onset.

And, above all, we wish to acknowledge the support of our wives, Judy and Linda.

Contents

"For me, the ultimate protest is to resist pain and disillusion, fascism and boredom. . . ."

FEDERICO FELLINI

Treat Your Ego in 4 Hours

The First Hour:
Brief Therapy Verbatim

What Do You Need?

Four hours from now, you will have an entirely new, fresh outlook on yourself and your life. You will be able to do much that you have never been able to do before. You will have strong, positive, feelings you have never felt before—toward yourself as well as others. You will see with new eyes, feel with new hands, master your problems in new, breakthrough ways. Most important, though, you will learn how to make yourself be whatever way *you* want to be.

We cannot guarantee all these benefits for every reader, of course. But developments in therapy over the years* and our own experience with Brief Therapy show that these life payoffs are within the reach of most people in four hours or slightly less. What we can give you are the

* See Scientific Appendix at the end of this book.

techniques that can provide greatly increased satisfaction from your life.

In our practice of psychiatry, we have found that people like to save time and money. So we strove to make Brief Therapy even more brief. We have designed this book to share our experience and that of others in a form that you can apply directly to your own life—starting four hours from right now.

Do you believe in magic? People do. Magic potions, good for anything that ails you . . . sold from the back of covered wagons. Cures at Lourdes. Oral Roberts. "Anacin for quick, three-way relief." Whatever. People look to healers for magic relief of life's ills. Healers in our own field use pills, electroshock, even psychosurgery (brain cutting). Psychoanalysts use more subtle magic: Four or five times a week, for maybe three to five years, of saying whatever comes into your mind without conscious censorship will liberate you! Imagine: Just talking freely, while resting on your back, to an intelligent and highly attentive listener will allow you to become a free spirit.

At last, the ultimate: a normal, healthy adult. (Whatever the hell that is!)

Or is the simplicity of a drug more your bag? If the green antidepressant didn't do it, perhaps the pink tranquilizer will. If Dr. Jones didn't figure you out, surely Dr. Smith will. If it isn't psychological, maybe it's medical. Everything was normal at your last checkup, but perhaps that famous Midwest clinic would be more thorough at diagnosing what ails you.

You're not hurting? So maybe you bought, borrowed, or stole this book because you believe in the magic of books: reading, knowledge, words. Printed words. It's not impossible that such magic exists. Within these covers could be the key to unlock some mysteries of life that lie within your grasp—some wizardry to help you emerge on a new level of self-mastery in just four hours of your time.

Maybe so. Maybe not. But $5.95 and four of your hours won't ruin your budget or waste much of your lifetime. So, what the hell?

What We Offer You

You can, in four hours, learn:

How to respect yourself
feel more important and successful
have more fun
get the most out of every day . . .
. . . just for you.

How to be well-loved
admired
appreciated . . .
. . . by those you love.

How to have the best control over your life
have ambitions and standards—and live up to them
make yourself be whatever way you *want to be . . .*
. . . because it's your life to use as you will.

What We Don't Offer You

peace at any price	vacations from life
Nirvana	endless treatment
spiritual transcendence	new bad names for people you don't like
effortless cures	another dull self-help book
rest and relaxation	

Here's our proposal. We have some wishes for you. Consider them *our* magic formulas for life. Dedicate yourself to them for these four hours with us. Can you? Will you? It's important, because if you can and do, you will have mastered the message of every wise man from Buddha to Freud, from Mohammed to Carl Rogers, from Jesus to . . .

BRIEF THERAPY MESSAGE #1

We want you to love yourself. We want you to take responsibility for your actions. We wish you selfish satisfaction of your needs.

Easy to write, to say, to read—almost trite. But every therapist, minister, counselor of any persuasion, the apostles of every messiah, all use techniques to change their parishioners, clients, or patients to satisfy needs, improve self-respect, and increase responsibility for all that one thinks, feels, says, and does.

We will try the same in the next three to four hours—only in a new, fast, breakthrough way. Our experience with individuals from every walk of life has given us confidence that you can benefit tremendously if you join us in the most fascinating of all life adventures. Many famous psychiatrists and research scientists have confirmed the effectiveness of making therapy brief.* Of course, we cannot guarantee the results for you. If we fail, try some other magic. You will have lost little.

So make yourself comfortable, *please!* Join us in this partnership to know you better. That's a good place to start. But perhaps you disagree. *Do you?*

Do you look forward to knowing yourself better? Or do you feel a twinge of discomfort . . . an indistinct but definite wish that we'd change the subject—as if some things about you might better remain unknown. You don't even know what they might be, but would rather "leave well enough alone."

Look, no one can hear us. We don't even know your name. Please trust us. Do risk going on. You can always stop later. Find out a little about how you are now. Find out what you really need. Because then . . . .

BRIEF THERAPY MESSAGE #2
You can make yourself be the way *you* want to be!

Yes, and in about three hours and fifty-four minutes from now!

You'll need a pencil and paper, a mirror, a clock, and

* References on these works can be found in the Scientific Appendix at the end of the book.

perhaps a tape recorder—all handy to your chair. Your undivided attention, your curiosity, and a bit of courage are all we ask.

Who are you? Do you know? Are you sure? How are you similar to other people, and how are you unique? Do other people seem to get more out of life? How much do you respect yourself? What are your needs, and are they being satisfied?

Maybe you're not so sure you know. Want to find out? Let's begin with why you are the way you are.

What Your Needs Are

Did you ever look at your life this way: Why do you get out of bed in the morning? Why do you go to work or clean the house? Why did you have children, let alone take care of them?

Why do you belong to organizations: PTA, bridge clubs, unions, and so forth? Why marry or have the affair, or live with a roommate (of the same or opposite sex)? Why do you do anything at all?

Right! Because you have needs. Everyone does: for food, air, shelter, water. Biological needs, necessary for survival. But more important, here and now, are your needs for involvement with other people. *Human* needs.

Biological needs, of course, are important, and can be threatened (by, for example, dire poverty, or when lost in the desert or trying to survive a mountain airplane crash).

In these situations, behavior can become very primitive. These biological needs go beyond our present scope. We do not have time in this rapid therapy to consider these extreme possibilities. Human needs, often more difficult to satisfy than biological ones, are of concern here.

BRIEF THERAPY MESSAGE #3
If you don't put your needs first—who will?

To get on top of your life, you first have to know what you need. Then learn how to get it. This may seem too simple, but you'd be surprised at how many people we've treated who had never thought of reducing their problems to this.

You may feel your problems have nothing to do with *your* needs. Do you feel you would be fine if only your wife (or husband) would stop complaining? Or if your lover would appreciate you? Or if you knew some different people? Or just had more money?

You may think unsatisfied needs are none of your doing, but try the following exercise anyway. You may change your mind—*and your life!*

Let's Pinpoint Basic Human Needs

What are some basic human needs? What do you need rom others (and they from you)?

First of all: *love!*

Corny? Maybe—maybe not. Let's see.

You are about to begin a series of simple exercises that will lead you through this book. These following will let you see how well you're managing your life. Just *read* the first one. Then *read* the example after it. Then *do* the exercise after that.

The "Love-Me" Exercise

Take a few minutes to complete the following questions. Allow yourself time to think and consider your feelings carefully. Rate yourself by the scales below:

		Your Score	Maximum Possible
First Choice?	Does the person I love the most *show* they love me more than anyone else?	____	5
(Score yourself from 0 [if they never show it] to 5 [if they always show their love to you].)			
Feel It?	How much do I feel the love they express?	____	3
(Score yourself from 0 [if you don't feel it] to 3 [if you feel it completely].)			
How Many?	How many people love me?	____	2
(Score yourself 0 [for none], 1 [for one], or 2 [for more than one other person].)			
	TOTAL	____	10

George did it like this:

He was a successful businessman in his early thirties who came for help with his excessive-smoking problem. Two packs a day . . . and he couldn't stop for long. He didn't want to do this exercise, but did it. This is how he rated himself.

> Well, I decided to give myself a 7. I love my wife very much. My wife loves me, I'm sure, but I'm also sure she loves the kids more. But my children love me at least as much as her. So, considering everything, I gave myself a 2, 3, and 2, for a total of 7.

Now, try it yourself.

		Your Score	Maximum Possible
First Choice? (Score yourself from 0 [if they never show it] to 5 [if they always show their love to you].)	Does the person I love the most *show* they love me more than anyone else?	____	5
Feel It? (Score yourself from 0 [if you don't feel it] to 3 [if you feel it completely].)	How much do I feel the love they express?	____	3
How Many? (Score yourself 0 [for none], 1 [for one], or 2 [for more than one other person].)	How many people love me?	____	2
	TOTAL	____	10

How well-loved are you? Check it out some more. Take another few minutes. This time, exclude all blood relatives, step-parents and step-children. Don't exclude your spouse! Again, pause, and candidly . . .

		Your Score	Maximum Possible
First Choice?	Does the person I love the most *show* they love me more than anyone else?	____	5
(Score yourself from 0 [if they never show it] to 5 [if they always show their love to you].)			
Feel It?	How much do I feel the love they express?	____	3
(Score yourself from 0 [if you don't feel it] to 3 [if you feel it completely].)			
How Many?	How many people love me?	____	2
(Score yourself 0 [for none], 1 [for one], or 2 [for more than one other person].)			
	TOTAL	____	10

Does all this seem a little brutal? We're sorry, but brutal honesty is not only the best policy for our purposes in these four hours—it is the *only* policy. We are being honest with you about what we think and feel, and we expect the same from you.

So reexamine your feelings. Can you say with complete comfort that you *feel* and *experience* and *have* a warm, thoroughly convincing awareness that at least one person other than parents, brothers, sisters, or children gives you their love as much as or more so than they share it with anyone else in the world?

Why do we exclude blood relatives? Does the love of parents mean nothing? Why ignore the heartwarming smiles of children, the pride of their accomplishments, their hugs, kisses, respect, devotion? Doesn't their love mean anything?

Of course it does! But children tend to take more than they return, and parental relations are never enough. A full adult life requires a partner (or two or more) without the handicap of generation gaps, of past history when one was a subordinate child and the other a responsible parent. The old obligations bind. Memories of discipline, sacrifice, or irresponsibility grate. It's inevitable.

Besides, we refuse to believe that only your parent or child could love you!

We ask you not to shun your family, but to risk sharing yourself with those who will love you freely, by choice, because of who you are *now,* rather than who you have been.

Do you freely love another, and are you ready to commit yourself to him/her? Can you share their feelings—both good and bad? Do you demonstrate your love in your behavior? Can you risk this loving commitment knowing that all relationships end by death, even if in no other way—knowing that the loss of a loved one is the most painful experience a human can have?

If you scored 8 or above, *congratulations!* It's such a

marvelous feeling to feel truly loving, lovable, and loved! (By the way, we also congratulate those who showed their love in ways you could believe while you were a young child.) Please feel free to skip to the next section, on control.

If you scored below 8, then you live with some feeling of emptiness and loneliness in your life. We understand the sadness—indeed, the anger—that echoes within you when you dwell on this emptiness. It is a very *human* feeling. People try to ignore it by activity, a brave front, perhaps even by deceiving themselves. Or they get lost in the negative experience, and feel abandoned, hopeless, helpless, and frustrated.

Perhaps you now face this emptiness for the first time. We admire your courage.

How Much Control Do You Have?

Before you start to learn how to get more love, check out your other needs:

Do you ever feel as if you were a log adrift on the sea . . . tossed and carried by wind and currents . . . lacking direction, purpose, or control of your day-to-day life?

How can you really tell?

You have a bureau or dresser in your bedroom; what do you keep in the upper drawer, left side? Can you picture those objects in your mind right now? How much gasoline do you have in the tank of your car? What is the day and date? What is your best friend's telephone number?

How much control do you have over your day-to-day life? Do you ever feel as if you were falling apart? Do other people seem to have things go their way more than you? Are you satisfied with your present job? How much can you count on your friends and family?

Answers to these questions—some trivial, others crucial—can tell you a lot about where you stand right now. Personal stability, balance, the feeling of having control over your life—these are essential to feeling whole and complete.

Belief about who your friends really are; that is, who you can and can't count on . . . and for what; memories of the past, and future plans; your place in the world; financial resources; job security—all of these contribute to your feelings of control.

Again, let's find out where you are now.

"Am I Really Living My Own Life?"

Score yourself according to your current feelings of how much influence you have over what happens to you. Take several minutes, and consider carefully before marking your score.

		Your Score	Maximum Possible
People Power	How much influence do I have over the people I love?	______	4

(Score yourself from 0 [for no influence] to 4 [for being able to count on them completely].)

Letting Go	Am I secure enough to be able to comfortably give up control (having an orgasm, letting other people get their way, etc.)?	____	4
(Score yourself from 0 [for never relaxing] to 4 [for "letting it all hang out" frequently].)			
What's Left?	Do I have as much control as I'd like to over other parts of my life?	____	2
(Score yourself from 0 [for powerless] to 2 [for feeling "in the driver's seat"].)			
	TOTAL	____	10

If you scored 8 or above, delightful! You may skip the next Brief Therapy Message. If you scored below 8, you feel trapped, weak, helpless, enslaved to some degree. You lack the exhilaration people usually feel when they are free to choose their future.

You will see as you go on that this feeling of security is actually a package of many beliefs: belief in yourself, principally. Control involves more than influence over your life situation (job, friends, marriage, money, etc.).

BRIEF THERAPY MESSAGE #4

Control involves belief in your freedom to choose. Freedom to choose involves the responsibility of choosing. Therefore, freedom, responsibility, and control are inseparable.

To feel in control, you must see that the state of your life exists because of choices you make. If you hold "fate," circumstances, your background, or "Karma" responsible, then you can of course complain; feel sorry for yourself; be cared for by friends, family, and physician; and seek refuge in bed, hospitals, or jails. But you trade freedom from responsibility for slavery and discontent.

Can you really believe that others would run your life better than you? Are you that weak? Can you respect anyone *that* trapped? That helpless? That ineffective?

If you want more influence over what happens to you, you must take responsibility for everything you do, say, think, feel.

How about it? Can you refuse someone when they ask you to do something? Or do you do things to avoid hurting others' feelings, while resentment and dissatisfaction grow within you?

Is control over your life worth risking your boss's displeasure or a loved one's anger? Are your feelings important enough to yourself to chance these risks?

We certainly hope so!

BRIEF THERAPY MESSAGE #5

If you don't take care of your needs, you can take care of nothing well.

So far, you have rated yourself on two of your basic needs: love and control. Now test yourself on two others: significance and fun.

Are You Significant?

Ask yourself: Is the world lucky I exist? Do I consider my family, friends, work associates, loved ones fortunate I am here on earth? Despite my faults and irritating habits, am I really a worthwhile, significant person? Am I glad to be me?

Let's check all this out.

The "I'm Glad to Be Me" Mirror Exercise

Take three minutes to look yourself in the eye, using a mirror. Say aloud how you feel about the person you see, without dropping your eyes. If possible, tape record what you say. (Remember, we are focusing on your feelings about yourself, not simply your personal appearance.)

Were you able to look yourself in the eye without dropping your gaze as you spoke? Did you run yourself down? Did you praise yourself in any way? Does pride embarrass you? Did you list more criticisms or "failures" than accomplishments?

Compare yourself to the following two people:

BILL (score: 9)

Hello, Bill. You really are a worthwhile guy. Mary is lucky to be your wife. John and Glen are lucky to have you as their dad. Sometimes you come on too strong, work too hard, are too critical, bitch too much, have too little fun, and have many other irritating qualities, but you are . . . [Breaks up laughing, looks away from mirror, looks back, then continues] . . . you are bright, sensitive, energetic, and warm. You are a superb engineer and fine skier. The world is indeed fortunate that you are here. You are as worthwhile as any person on earth. I am glad to be you!

Artificial? Maybe. But maybe not. Most people can say almost anything to a mirror except something nice about themselves. People are trained not to "boast." Talking to your mirror image is a very good test of how worthwhile you feel, and helps to develop comfort with improved self-worth.

We gave Bill in the above example a 9. He was very good at listing positive things about himself. Like many of us, though, he listed more bad things than good . . . as if he shouldn't be *too* proud. So we gave him a 9 out of 10.

BOB (score: 4)

Hello, Bob. How are you doing? . . . [Looks down at floor] . . . You're O.K., I guess . . . [Looks up for a moment, then down again] . . . There's some people who aren't as worthwhile as you. I guess you're all right. Betty says she loves you, so there must be something good about you . . .

Bob had told us earlier that his problem was that he had no energy. No wonder! Who can feel energetic when they also feel worthless? And who would want to do anything with someone who feels so worthless? Perhaps those who feel inadequate themselves?

Bob had difficulty saying anything good about himself while looking in the mirror. He did say that somebody else thinks he's worthwhile—but that's a far cry from feeling it himself. Besides, how can Bob feel anyone really loves someone so undeserving as he sees himself?

The purpose of this sequence of exercises is to show you how much you are getting and how much you could get. So now take your performance from the "I'm Glad to Be Me" Mirror Exercise and score yourself.

The "How I Rate Myself" Exercise

Take several minutes to score yourself on your self-concept, your feelings of self-worth, your self-respect. Pause and consider carefully before scoring yourself.

		Your Score	Maximum Possible
You	Do I respect myself as much as I'd like to?	_____	5
(Score yourself from 0 [for feeling worthless] to 5 [for feeling the world's lucky you're here!].)			
New Ones	Am I confident that people who meet me will respect me?	_____	3
(Score yourself from 0 [for "knowing" they won't respect you] to 3 [for having complete confidence that you deserve their respect].)			
Old Ones	Do others respect me as I'd like them to?	_____	2
(Score yourself from 0 [if you feel they don't] to 2 [if you *know* they do].)			
	TOTAL	_____	10

If you scored 8 or above by *honestly* expressing high self-respect in the mirror exercise, it follows that you must radiate a sense of well-being that attracts other healthy, vigorous, competent, loving people. You are a delight to know; others want to share experiences with you. You don't need to use, sacrifice, or buy others to attract them. To paraphrase the title of a recent best-seller, "you are your own best friend."

If you scored below 8, you have some work to do in the next hours. Will you risk developing increased self-respect, with our help?

Do you see that all your feelings about yourself flow from this?

Do you feel you must earn your worthwhileness?

Do you believe you must be successful, perfect, or better than others to be worthwhile?

When you were growing up, were you loved just because you existed? Did you have to perform extremely well to earn your parents' love? When you performed well, did you receive hugs and kisses—or were "nice" words your only reward? Worse yet, did you learn that only delinquent behavior could get your parents' attention? Even that would be preferable to the most horrible of all experiences . . . to be *ignored* by those you care about most!

BRIEF THERAPY MESSAGE #6

Oh, to feel loved *just* because you exist! That's the best there is!

Yes, you *can* feel worthwhile just because you exist. No, you don't need to earn your worthwhileness. You can be free!

If you have the courage to risk new attitudes and behavior, we'll help you feel worthwhile and lovable. You deserve respect as much as anyone else on this earth!

BRIEF THERAPY MESSAGE #7
Once you recognize your worth, you can spend your time using it rather than having to work at earning it.

And then, finally, that step-child of the Puritan ethic:

Fun. Fun? Yes, Fun!

When did you last play as a child might?

Do you set aside time for fun, play, and enjoyable exercise?

Do you have to earn your pleasure?

Do you have to wait until the evening or weekend, when work is done?

When did you last allow yourself an unbridled laugh or exuberant scream?

Imagine yourself unashamedly relaxing nude in a hot whirlpool bath. Imagine yourself having a massage by an expert. Do you regularly lose yourself in sexual pleasure?

Do you place a high priority on new and different pleasures —sensual or otherwise? We hope you feel you deserve all the fun and pleasure you can arrange! Do you? Now try. . .

The "Fun and Frolic" Exercise

Score yourself on the question "Do I have fun in my life now?" Again, take several minutes to consider carefully before marking your score.

		Your Score	Maximum Possible
Fun for Fun's Sake	Do I feel I have to earn the fun I have?	____	5
(Score yourself from 0 [if you never feel you deserve fun] to 5 [if you play on a regular basis].)			
Your Fun or Their Fun?	Do I get to have my choice over the kind of fun I have?	____	3
(Score yourself from 0 [if you always "go along"] to 3 [if you plan and lead the fun frequently].)			
Want More Fun?	Can I have fun by myself?	____	2
(Score yourself from 0 [if you hate being alone] to 2 [for regular enjoyment of solitary pursuits].)			
	TOTAL	____	10

If you score above 8, you enjoy yourself, you don't miss out on things you would like to do, you get the fun you need. You are not enslaved by the Judeo-Christian work ethic.

If you scored below 8, you deprive yourself.

Why?

Don't you deserve to enjoy yourself?

You say you feel guilty dropping everything? You think relaxation is time wasted? Why must work be completed for you to feel free to enjoy yourself?

Perhaps you can have fun, but *only* after a few drinks or marijuana. Do you use alcohol, tranquilizers, or grass to "relax" your conscience? Do you permit the happy-go-lucky child to emerge (temporarily) only if intoxicated?

O.K. But watch out! If you can let go only while drugged, you are on the path of habituation, or even addiction (in the case of booze and tranquilizers). More about this later.

BRIEF THERAPY MESSAGE #8

Make play a high priority and you enrich your entire life.

In the past forty minutes you have reviewed your current life to check out how well you fill your personal and social needs. Are you satisfied now that you are taking care of yourself in a healthy way?

If not, there are ways to take care of your needs better; ways to make your personal style work for you.

Do You Really Know Your Style?

What is *your* personal style? How do you handle new experiences? people? problems? How well does your style meet your needs? Could it work better?

Personal styles are the ways we make use of ourselves. They are ways to get what we want; ways to avoid what we don't want. Styles start with the genes we were born with, and our early experiences. As children we learn styles from other people. We learn, but not always what works best. We learn by our experiences with what happens to surround us.

Reflect on your early life. Can you see how you were affected by important adults in your childhood? A useful exercise, but not enough. Even if you completely understood how you developed, it's how you behave each day *now* that maintains your style.

Of course, styles are as unique as every individual. Your style defines your life. Within each culture some are more popular than others. But always each style is based on what is most important to a person: most desired or most feared.

Some styles work better than others. So, how about yours?

Good Styles and Bad Styles

Styles that don't work well are those that make you give up needs—give up love, give up fun, give up self-respect—when you don't have to.

BRIEF THERAPY MESSAGE #9

Brief Therapy is one way of learning how to get back what you may have given up—*quickly!*

Styles that work come in all shapes and sizes. They all take care of needs. When your style works, you can have security and still keep self-respect. You can get personal significance and not give up on love or fun.

Everyone has seen people who have styles that work. They look content, self-confident, happy, and well-loved, and they run their own show. Can a winning style be learned? Of course it can.

First of all, find out how well your style works for you in the . . .

"Who's Working for Whom?" Exercise

How well does your current personal style take care of your needs? Pause and consider carefully before marking your score.

		Your Score	Maximum Possible
Satisfaction	Right now my basic human needs are well taken care of.	______	5
(Score yourself from 0 [if your needs aren't taken care of at all] up to 5 [if they are completely satisfied].)			
Risk Taking	Given the choice of new situations to take care of needs or stay-		

	ing with habits, I'd take a chance.		3
(Score yourself from 0 [if you stick to unsatisfying habits] up to 3 [if you try new solutions often].)			
Responsibility	I act like it's nobody else's responsibility to take care of me.		2
(Score yourself from 0 [if you don't] up to 2 [if you always do].)			
	TOTAL		10

If you scored above 8, your style works well. You even experiment with new experiences to take care of your needs. Most people admire you and wonder how you manage to be so satisfied and fulfilled as you look. You have chosen friends, loved ones, and occupation well. Congratulations.

If you scored below 8, your style doesn't work too well for you. You may feel caught up in the same day-to-day routine, powerless to change it. You may be working to keep up a style that doesn't take care of your needs.

Yet you obviously have courage, because you have already been willing critically to evaluate who you are. We appreciate how difficult that is! *Anyone who has done this can successfully complete the rest of this Brief Therapy.*

What Habits Do You Really Need?

Styles can sometimes be just habits, patterns that you repeat in your life again and again. The same arguments, the same hurts, the same frustrations.

It's tough getting out of a rut. We are all basically "creatures of habit." We act pretty much the same each day. And why not? With habits, you don't have to put out so much energy. Doing the same old thing may not be much fun, but it sure is easy. It's the line of least resistance.

And often other people want us to stay much the same. That's what most human relationships are based on. We all expect our families and friends to have about the same feelings, the same likes and dislikes, each time we see them. We might be worried that something was wrong if they suddenly spoke, dressed, or walked differently. Habits can identify people, help make them truly individual.

Changing Your Habits to Master a Changing World (Or, If You Must Sit on the Escalator, Don't Think You Won't Move)

If only the whole world stayed the same every day, then styles made of habits would be fine. But the world does change. The unexpected fades into the commonplace. There's always something happening, and things won't stop. Call it stress, future shock, daily tension—it doesn't matter. From our marriages to our jobs, there's pressure to decide how to act in changing situations.

For some, the decision is to give up. They stay the same, don't take any chances, and sit on their dull escalator. Others meet change and master it by a style that works—for them, and for their loved ones, too.

BRIEF THERAPY MESSAGE #10
You can make your style work by thinking about your needs more and using habits less.

Think of Yourself

You may wonder, "If I make my human needs for love, security, significance, and fun most important, wouldn't I be selfish?"

That's right:

SELFISH
SELFISH
SELFISH
SELFISH!!!

The "Selfish" Exercise

Simply say, "I want to be selfish," five times. Don't score yourself. Now, selfishly take a ten-minute break.

Selfish. It's kind of a moral insult, a cultural myth—as though you're a better person if you're not selfish. Through our studies of people we found this just isn't true. By trying not to be selfish, people often succeed only in becoming impossible to live with.

Would you rather be frustrated, complaining, irritable, hostile, unsatisfied? Don't kid yourself—trying not to be selfish does not make you more lovable.

Of the people who try never to think of themselves, Jane was typical. She was depressed, frustrated, and felt that people avoided her. She was angry that she never could do what she wanted to.

"Nobody can call me selfish.

"You shouldn't love yourself first, it's just not right. Now, if somebody appreciates you, that's one thing, but people can't go around loving *themselves.* I admit I'm frustrated a lot, especially when my family doesn't notice how I sacrifice for them. And I'd like to go skiing again, but I can't, haven't in years, because of them. But they need me, you know. I also admit that I nag too much, but how could thinking about myself make anything better?"

What do you want better? For her, better was giving up the control she had to make her family feel terrible. They were all sick of hearing about how she wanted to go skiing. Instead of waiting for them to do something, she did it herself, and they began to like her more.

BRIEF THERAPY MESSAGE #11

If you can't love yourself, you can't love anyone else.

Three hours left to go. By now you know how to test your needs. You have a better idea of how loved and secure you are, how much you respect yourself, and how much fun you have. Is your style working for you? Or are you caught up in habits that keep you unsatisfied?

Maybe right now you are hurting: feeling sad, frustrated, just not very satisfied about where your life is going. That's all right to feel if you want your life to be different. People don't change when they feel good. You're heading toward making your life the way you want it to be. If you want to change, keep going.

The Second Hour: *How's This for a Change?*

Is It Time for You to Change?

Do you ever ask yourself: When should I

start listening to others?
start expressing myself?
stop giving in?
stop smoking?
stop overeating?
stop feeling sorry for myself?
start having fun?
stop trying too hard?
start trying harder?

The basic questions are really simple: How can I know *when? When* should I keep doing the same thing? *When* should I do something different?

Some people seem to know. They're always one jump

ahead of everyone else. They seem able to anticipate the problems that knock others down. How do they do it? Can they foretell the future?

In our studies of people who have a grip on their lives, we found that the same rules apply. From the successful businessman satisfied with his relationships and projects to the wilderness man living with his friends and nature, identical rules hold. Simple rules. Here's how to apply these rules to yourself:

Change the way you act when you aren't getting what you want, when you find something that's better for you than what you have.

What you will learn in this hour is how to check out whether you *are* getting what you want, and how to tell whether another way is better than what you have now.

Have You Been Getting Enough?

You already know how to find out your needs. Have your scores from Hour 1 handy, and go over them again. That's the fastest way to know exactly how well you're doing. But there is another way—a way to discover how you *feel*.

Are you dissatisfied? frustrated? disgusted? hurting? tired? depressed? fed up? tense? anxious? If you feel bad often enough, you will think about changing. Maybe that's the reason you are reading this book: psychological pain; the feeling that *things just are not right*.

That feeling comes in many shapes and sizes. It's probably different for everyone. Yet, pain always is the reason why people change what they do. What you need to find out is how to respond to discomfort before it becomes severe or even overwhelming.

After all, pain is a message that there is something wrong. Right? If you touch a hot iron, your body says to you, "Ouch, don't *do* that!" Yet people who have the sense to avoid touching a hot iron put up with pain which is much worse! That's a shame, because pain is a message: *Take care of yourself.*

When you hurt with psychological pain, you should get the message. And the first thing to understand is the kind and severity of your pain. Here's a checklist:

Discomfort. Mild frustration or annoyance, boredom, lack of enthusiasm. Usually a dull, aching feeling that something is wrong. The easiest kind of pain to "put up with," but it takes all the fun out of life. Very, very common.

Displeasure. Frustration with dissatisfaction. Usually comes from repeated fights with another person. Typically, this occurs in a marriage where the partners stay together even though they argue almost constantly and destructively. Just as bad are relationships with chronic but unexpressed disagreements and dissatisfaction. Being able to get away from the job or the other person can make this barely tolerable.

Outright Pain. Psychological pain with unavoidable frustration, tension, anxiety, anger, depression, hopelessness. People cannot ignore this for long, and will usually try to escape somehow or seek help.

Panic. The worst sort of pain; accompanied by disruption

of usual behavior. Usually caused by overwhelming misfortune or frustration. The reactions to this are usually highly visible and nearly impossible to tolerate at all.

How much do you have to hurt before *you* change?

When you're not taking care of your needs, you start hurting. To get more control over your life, learn to respond to the hurting as soon as it begins.

The simplest way to start is to test yourself.

The "Do I Hurt Badly Enough Yet?" Exercise

		Your Score	Maximum Possible
How Much?	How much pain have I been feeling recently?	______	4
(Score from 0 [for panic] to 4 [for occasional discomfort].)			
How Often?	How frequently am I hurting?	______	4
(Score from 0 [for constantly] to 4 [for rarely].)			
How Hopeless?	When I hurt, do I feel as if anything can be done to get relief?	______	2
(Score from 0 [for hopeless] to 2 [for secure].)			
	Total Possible Score	______	10

If your score was 8 or above, pain does not dominate your life. You can experience what discomfort you have without becoming demoralized. Pain does not keep you from getting what you want.

If your score was below 8, pain is getting in your way. You may often think about your pain; you may wonder what you should do. The way you feel shows very definitely that you should change.

When the Grass Looks Greener Someplace Else

To tell whether you should change the way you act involves comparing what you *have* to what you might *get*.

Even if you were completely miserable before you started reading this book, *don't rush to change!* Think about it this way: After all, you *do* have one thing going for you: You know what you have. Your life is fairly consistent. You can tell what to expect. To change, you often must give up things you take for granted.

O.K., so your life might be unsatisfactory now. You may lack some self-respect, for instance. But you enjoy the comfort of a predictable life.

You do have choices. But are they worthwhile?

You want to stand up for yourself in arguments more?

. . . Are you sure? You might lose some people you thought were friends.

You want to be more intimate with specific people?

. . . Are you sure? They might put demands on you.

The best way to figure out whether it's worth changing any part of the way you act is to find out first what you can get out of it. Any way you act, anything you do, has costs as well as benefits for you.

Here are some choices:

Wear a coat and tie to apply for a new job?

Benefit: the promise of regular income
Cost: might be uncomfortable; might sacrifice your individuality to appease the boss

Stop giving in to avoid fighting with someone you love?

Benefit: might get love, self-respect, and more control
Cost: might lose your loved one

Whatever you do, you get something but you also pay for it in some way. Obvious? Not necessarily. Relationships (marriage, friendship, love) do have obvious benefits and costs. But try to give up a bad habit with a *hidden* benefit and you'll soon learn why you kept the habit.

We find that people who "can't" change their habits often have that difficulty because they don't see what they get out of them. Which is why it's so important to find out what you have before you decide to change.

How to Escape: "Good" Ways and "Bad" Ways

Escapes. We all need them. We all use them. Why? Because the things we do don't always work to get us what we want. Then we feel discomfort, displeasure, even pain. Modern psychiatrists call this being in *crisis.*

To attempt to escape when you feel pain couldn't be more natural. If you don't try to escape, you're foolish, "crazy," or both.

As with most other things in life, escapes are of two kinds: good and bad. Think of some escapes. Make a list. How many escapes can you think of? And what kind?

Now compare your list with ours:

suicide/homicide
mental illness
physical illness
alcohol (to excess)
drugs (tranquilizers, sedatives, stimulants)
sleeping (to excess)
masturbating (to excess)
eating (to excess)
working (to excess)
daydreaming (to excess)
worrying (without taking action)

Your list is more complete? Excellent! We're on the same wave length. Now we'd like to add the following to our list:

rest
recreation
vacations
entertainment (theaters, TV, etc.)
even the occasional drug, like alcohol, to help the mind and body relax

How can you tell a good escape from a bad one?

Bad escapes reduce your discomfort for the moment—but make it likely that you will emerge with less satisfaction and lowered self-respect.

Good escapes reduce your pain while leaving you in good shape.

A better name for the very best escapes is "solutions." They not only relieve discomfort in the long run; they leave you satisfied and proud. When people in pain (crisis) consult psychiatrists, these are the solutions the "shrinks" hope to work out.

What's "Excessive," Anyway?

Obviously suicide, homicide, and illness are bad escapes. But what do we mean by drinking, sleeping, masturbating, eating, working, or, indeed, any other activity "to excess"?

Easy. It's when you eat (sleep, masturbate, drink, etc.) more than your therapist!

Not fair? O.K. We'll suspend religious, ethical, and personal values. How, then, can you decide whether any particular behavior is a bad escape, a good one, or even an excellent solution?

Consult an "expert"?

Not at all necessary. Simply apply the following yardstick:

BRIEF THERAPY MESSAGE #12
Will (does) the behavior satisfy you and increase your self-respect?

This question lets you evaluate your current behavior. More important, we'll show you later how to use it to plan some positive changes.

How about an example?

Jerry gets along being a nice, easy-going, pleasant fellow who gets the job done. He just received a promotion over five of his buddies, effective in three months. Now he must adjust to being a supervisor responsible for his five friends' output. He begins to worry that he might have overstepped his abilities and reached his optimal level of incompetence (the Peter Principle). He stays at work longer, to learn how to handle his increased responsibilities. He becomes tense at home, less loving; he receives less from his wife and children. His fellow workers begin to see him less like a buddy and more like a boss. He feels less loved and less in control. He worries that he will fail. He feels worthless. He has less fun. He feels pain. He is in crisis.

Jerry could decide to talk over his situation with his family, co-workers, and boss. He might find new friends, or work out matters with his old colleagues. He could plan his decreased leisure time better so that the quality of his family time improved despite the quantity's decreasing. He might convince his boss to provide him with management training . . . and so forth. All these possible choices involve changing his passive, non-confronting, easy-going style to some degree.

He might select a good escape, such as a long weekend to relax, play and talk over the situation with his wife and family. Like most solutions, these would take much more planning and effort than simple escape would.

Or he might choose a bad escape, by drinking, taking tranquilizers, quitting his job, getting sick, sleeping away his spare time, eventually even having a nervous breakdown or breaking the law in order to get caught—or, indeed, attempting suicide if life becomes sufficiently dissatisfying.

Do we mean to imply he would deliberately arrange to become an alcoholic, or to become physically or mentally ill?

Of course not! But if the discomfort is sufficiently severe, his resistance will drop, and eventually he will become sick in some way.

By now you see that everything you do has a payoff. Whether it is increased satisfaction and self-respect, "sacrificial" acts in the futile hope that someone will reward you someday, or simply escape from pain, you do what you do because you want the benefits.

To put it simply:

BRIEF THERAPY MESSAGE #13
"Sick" habits (bad escapes) have their good points, too.

Think about the habits that everybody says are undesirable. Even those supposedly sick habits have benefits. It's just that the costs are so large. Those habits can be used occasionally. Some people make them a way of life. We call them:

Careers in Failure

Here's how to recognize some of the most common of these careers.

"I'm not too well, you know . . ." Definitely a favorite. Includes obesity, depression, alcoholism, and other addictions; physical invalidism.

"All work and no play. Lord knows I try!" Also quite popular. This career in failure includes *workaholics* and *work addicts*; buying self-respect exclusively through work; putting off pleasure; striving after possessions that never seem to satisfy.

"Not now, but someday." Somewhat less popular as a complete way of life, but often played along with such other careers as: "It's not up to me," "It will be better some day," or "Can't do anything differently."

Careers in failure. They all are seemingly "bad" problems. Yet each has its hidden benefits. Let's look at some.

When You Live off the Fat of the Land

Take obesity. How do you get overweight? Genetic physical predisposition or not, somewhere along the line you *have* to overeat to be fat. (Why not, it's the great American pastime!) Even with physical disease, what you do with yourself—whatever your limitations—is largely up to you. If you tend to be fat, changing how much you eat is still the fastest way to change how much you weigh.

What can you get by being overweight? And what's the cost?

Here's how to count up the costs and benefits of obesity:

Costs: As you get fatter you will . . .

be less attractive

have trouble finding clothes that fit

be ill more frequently (diabetes, heart disease, arthritis, etc.)

stay at home more

get even fatter

have fewer friends

lose self-respect

All right—*everyone* knows what's bad about being fat. What could possibly be good about it?

Plenty!

Benefits: As you eat more, you can . . .

get protection from demanding relationships (This works better and better as you get fatter and fatter. Who would want anything from someone *that* fat? If you don't attract anyone, you needn't fear rejection.)

get pity (Although people may dislike you or find your weight problem funny, or sad, few will ever openly confront you. Most people will feel sorry for you. They will spare your feelings, and avoid openly making you angry or sad.)

get a very satisfying and rewarding fantasy life (So nice just to sit back, have a little something to eat, and dream about how beautiful, successful, happy you could easily have been if only you weren't so fat . . . and never have to risk failure, or the demands and expectations made on those who succeed! The satisfaction of knowing that anyone who cares about [loves?] you must really love *you*, since they must ignore your appearance. Many people make this strange distinction between "themselves" and their appearance. As if "my body is not a part of who I am!")

get instant and constant safety in the protective envelope of fat—and the food tastes so good! (You can get enormous pleasure from sticking things in your mouth. And it's only as far as the next supermarket, refrigerator, or drive-up food store.)

always have something to talk about! (Even if you don't like talking about your "weight problem," you can talk about your latest diet.)

Obesity, alcoholism, or other physical problems that produce invalidism can greatly influence how other people treat you. So you see: Making a career of these illnesses isn't just having a disease. It's *using* obesity or depression or physical illness to remind everyone around you just how sick you are, how little they should expect, how much you need to be cared for, even if you can't expect and don't deserve to be loved!

No question about it: Bad habits have many hidden benefits. The better you do at recognizing them, the better off you'll be.

Which is why we insist that people with obesity or other illnesses honestly consider the benefits they get from their current style.

Who hasn't held back from expressing frustration to a sick person in order not to bother them? Or gone out of their way to help someone who is "ill"? The benefits of invalidism are very real.

Yet people with careers in failure don't deliberately decide one day to become sick. To become obese, you don't say to yourself, "Gee, I'd like to be fat—that way people will not expect much from me." It doesn't work that way, as everybody knows.

Rather: Careers in failure develop sneakily, bit by bit. Maybe you're unsure of yourself. You want to be liked, but don't know how to handle people as well as you'd like to. What can you do?

If you feel uptight about it and you find that overeating feels good, you can keep eating. And it helps take your mind off your problems.

Worries about whether people would appreciate you will fade away as you get fatter and fatter. Fat makes you feel safe. Lonely, but safe in your hopeless, invalid state.

Even though you are miserable, your career in failure

might be too good to give up. Really. Have you ever thought of one of your problems in this way?

Careers in failure based on illness are very popular. An endless parade of TV commercials caters to millions who have retreated from life into careers of greater or lesser invalidism—the millions who buy those tension-headache/upset-stomach medicines, for example.

Remember that careers in failure come in all varieties and severities. Maybe you are not feeling sick constantly. But do you use the benefits of "not feeling well tonight"?

Count these benefits right now. Then count the costs.

People have changed mild and undramatic problems by these methods, too. Even problems that aren't usually thought of as problems.

Like working . . .

Help for "Workaholics"

Working constantly. Putting off pleasure. "Workaholics": work addicts. Feeling that you must achieve and perform constantly. It's as common a career in failure as obesity or other illnesses.

To show you what we mean, we'll tell you about John (with his permission, of course).

John was a topnotch executive—with a career in failure. Impossible? Let's see.

He was appreciated by his bosses. Acquaintances found him likable and energetic. What concerned him was how seldom he was with his wife and children. And he never had a chance to do what *he* wanted to do. He was frequently sought after to help friends and associates, and couldn't say "no." He started work early, finished late, and took a bulging attaché case of papers home every night. Appointments and contracts piled up on him. He almost never could take a vacation.

He wanted to work less. When his family doctor told him his heart would be giving him big trouble if he didn't slow down, he began to get the message. But when he started to ease off, he felt depressed and worried.

He said, "I could stop working completely, but slowing down is impossible! I've got just too much to do."

So we had him list what he was getting and how much it cost him. He was a very successful businessman, highly skilled at computing costs and expenses. Yet he had never even thought about the cost-versus-profits balance sheet of his very own personal life: what *he* was getting out of all that work.

John's lists looked like this:

Costs: What working too much costs me:
can't enjoy my family
no weekends for myself
increased chance of heart attack
feel trapped by my job/my fixed expenses
never really get the self-respect I try for
feel like I'm on a treadmill, not getting anywhere
feel like I can't stop or I'll lose everything.

Then he listed what he did get.

Benefits: What working so much does for me:

having people depend on me makes me feel important and worthwhile
I never have to be alone and confront who I am and what I feel
I feel I do some things very well
I never have to wonder what to do with myself
many people admire me for what I do
If I underwork I might lose my job, my security
I keep a safe distance from the problems of my family and friends by being busy
I never have to openly say "no," because I always have other commitments as excuses
I feel better when I'm working
when I'm idle, I feel meaningless

John's lists made him decide to change. The benefits were good, but he felt he could get them in other ways. So he started to *fake it* (you'll learn how in Hour 3) and act *as if* he didn't have to work so much. This enabled him gradually to decrease his commitments.

He would call for reinforcements from his family and friends; reward himself with fishing trips for *not* being helpful or going out of his way; allow others to compliment him without feeling as if he had to earn it; learn how not to be helpful and have his self-respect without earning it. (Details on these and other solutions will be found in Hour 3.)

That's how John changed. You can do the same. Find

out first whether it's worth your while to change. If it is, then use the methods you will learn in Hour 3. But before you change, be sure to figure out the costs and benefits.

How to Figure the Costs and Benefits of Changing

Now that you have learned a little about escapes, solutions, and careers in failure, you can find out what you are getting right now. You know how well you are satisfying your needs, how well your style works for you. You also know how much pain you have from what you do. You might even have started to treat yourself differently already.

But *should* you start a change? Should you begin another way of acting?

Find out by listing the costs and benefits of changing or not changing. To make it easier, we made a list of common benefits and costs of staying the same. Check out our list first.

Benefits of not *changing:*

avoid responsibilities, anger, demands
takes little effort to stay the same
often pleasurable (drinking in alcoholism, eating in obesity, etc.)
familiar situations—perhaps painful, but no risks
respectable to be "sick" or disabled
less pressure from people if you stay the same
you don't threaten others, you're not competing in the game of life . . . you are a victim, a spectator, an onlooker . . . others will ignore you, or take care of

you . . . but they won't hurt you . . . you aren't worth the effort

And the typical costs:

costs of not *changing:*

loneliness, frustration, tension, pain
decreased self-respect, fun, satisfaction
others are in control
feelings of boredom, meaninglessness, of being trapped, of hypocrisy in trying to please others but not yourself

Now get down to the nitty-gritty of finding out if it's worth changing for you.

The "What's in It for Me? (And How Much Will It Cost?)" Exercise

Make a list of all costs and benefits of any behavior you are thinking about changing. Take a half-hour and make the list complete.

If the benefits of your current style honestly add up to more than the costs, then stay the way you are now; or examine both lists to see if you can maneuver things to decrease the cost of changing while increasing the benefits.

If the costs now are greater than the benefits, consider changing.

Fine, but what *can* you do differently?

How Do You Want to Be?

When to change?
When you hurt!

What to change?
Self-defeating escapes.

Change to what?

Remember that any change involves effort and risk. But the different possible ways of behaving are literally infinite. You may not yet see many of these ways, but they're there.

How can you select the best new ways?

The best ways are the ones that promise enough payoff. Start with . . .

The "To Mine Own Self Be True" Exercise (Part I)

Right now, make a written list of how you would have to behave to increase your self-respect.

Rules:

1. *They must increase your self-worth.*
2. *Be selfish, not sacrificing.*
3. *Be specific.*
4. *Confine yourself to things you can do this week.*
5. *Make them reasonable.*
6. *List efforts to be made,* not *results to be accomplished.*
7. *Include work, socializing, and playing.*
8. *Make them changes in actual* behavior—*not changes in* feelings.

For example:

Work:	complete overdue work project
	negotiate for a raise
	express long-overdue honest anger at supervisor, peer, subordinate
Socializing:	pursue one new friendship
	show him/her love more directly
	ask him/her for more direct loving
Play:	enroll in skiing/scuba school
	schedule double the playtime that you've been getting
	plan one fun-filled evening with the person(s) you love the most.

What you wind up with is simply an idea list. You are not obligated to carry out anything you list!

But do take at least fifteen minutes to list at least three changes for your day-to-day behavior.

Don't worry if you know you can't make these changes right now because you don't feel up to it. We'll help you with that very shortly.

Take a chance. Make the list. No one will know but you!

If you are reading this paragraph without having made the list, we're not surprised. Most of our clients also fear even considering changes that would involve risks—even if they would profit greatly from the changes. Someday, when you hurt enough—or when a friend, or therapist, or book is convincing enough—or when your courage grows, you'll make that list.

But if you did make the list (and according to the rules), then you made the first giant step toward improving your life. You are making our efforts in authoring this book worth it and you're ready for . . .

The "To Mine Own Self Be True" Exercise (Part II)

Take your list from Part I.

Be certain the rules were followed. Many people list sacrificial, society-approval-seeking, vague or unreasonable suggestions for themselves.

Examine each change for advantages and disadvantages.

Skilled therapists often ask their patients to fantasize the worst possible consequences of a feared event or change in behavior. Being skilled therapists, we ask you to do that very thing with each of the changes you just listed. The worst possible, please!

Now eliminate from your list any behavior that might really lead to a result you feel you could not tolerate.

If you still have at least one item left—great!

If you no longer have a list, don't even consider changing your ways of living. Be satisfied with what you've got. You *can't* tolerate the possible results of changing. Continue reading only out of curiosity. You won't change.

You Only Go Around Once in Life

It comes down to your making a choice between comfort and freedom. Comfort means no risks . . . and living with the discomfort you know so well. No more fun than you're having now . . . and no more intimacy. No more passion . . . and no more excitement. No deeper friendships . . . and no new experiences . . . nothing other than what you've had up to now.

Many people would "rather bear those ills we've had, than fly to others we know not of."

Hamlet knew that death is the final comfort. Death comes guaranteed. But why play dead while you're still alive? Why avoid risks, wasting the only chance you're likely to have?

How do you go about taking chances?

We thought you'd never ask. We're glad you did, because we've got answers.

Work, play, and love in new ways this week and this weekend. It's as simple as that.

Of course, some people choose extreme risks to gain peak excitement: defying death in sky diving, motorcycle or car racing. High payoffs in the form of money, fame, great excitement, temporary victories over death are possible. Happily, most risks involve less permanent, less irreversible consequences. The choice, as always, is yours. Why not take your pick?

(Some people, indeed, risk death through suicide attempts [gestures?], to gain sympathy and/or punish others for their own despair. If death occurs, then they have managed to get "even" and punish those "others." If they survive, perhaps the world—impressed by the action—will take better care of them. But by the very act of self-destruction, regardless of the result, self-respect evaporates. No payoff is worth that!)

What we're talking about is . . .

BRIEF THERAPY MESSAGE #14
Take reasonable risks that may improve need satisfaction and increase self-worth.

Fine, but how?

We hoped you'd ask!

BRIEF THERAPY MESSAGE #15
This week *work, play, love* in new ways—ways you may have wished to try but were afraid to risk for fear of embarrassment, rejection, failure.

How?

By risking, now! In small steps or, at times, in large leaps.

Fear is the enemy of freedom and fulfillment. Fear, like dandruff, cannot be eliminated, only controlled.

Some suggestions:

At work, say what you've wanted to say; try the new approach you've considered for so long.

At play, begin the new hobby. If you're a follower, lead for a change. If a leader, take a back seat this week. Try a new sex technique.

Love. Try sharing some feelings you've withheld. Share a positive and a negative feeling with someone you care about, and do it honestly, directly.

Try just one new approach in each of these three key aspects of your life this week and you will have grown more than most people manage in a decade!

Our Guarantee

If you risk behaving in a more self-respecting way, you absolutely will feel better about yourself—*whatever the results.*

The Bonus

You might even get a good or best-possible result.

Now you've decided what to do differently. In the next hour, you'll learn precisely how.

The Third Hour:
Stoppers and Movers

You've completed two hours—looked at your style and thought about change. Either you're not entirely satisfied with your life, or your desire to grow pushes you to read on. Fine.

You can have changes make your life better. Working with all sorts of people, we've seen a few simple principles that really work. They can work for you, too.

First, share our view of a creative life:

Accept responsibility for satisfying your needs
Build self-respect
Change bad escapes to good ones

Why a "creative life"? Because coming up with new solutions to everyday demands is a creative life. The worst style is one that is entirely habit—especially, senseless repetition of failure. (Which is a definition of neurosis by the way.)

Want to change? There are some steps you must take.

Clearly, to avoid responsibility for *you* by blaming others (or "circumstances") will keep you tied down to your dissatisfaction. Taking responsibility frees you.

Can you accept both credit and blame? Criticism for your less-than-perfect performances? Praise for your successes? It's the price of getting control of your life.

Hold on a minute! We've already covered that ground. You've already started doing something about your life, *now!* You've accepted that changing your actions changes your self-image and feelings. But there's more to it.

BRIEF THERAPY MESSAGE #16
To think differently is to think differently, but to behave differently is to *be* different.

All right! Now put it into action!

You've already decided what needs aren't satisfied. You've examined your style and chosen behavior you'd prefer. You've carefully examined the advantages and disadvantages of your current style. You've looked at pros and cons of new behaviors. You're primed and waiting for some direction, some cues, some clues, some magic to make your dreams realities in the brief time we promised.

How to Get Ready to Change

Say you decide to change something about your life: the way you act, the way someone treats you, the way you feel. What can you do to get ready?

We find that people who have a grip on their lives treat themselves differently than people who feel defeated. To be able to change any part of your life, you have to feel as if you can do it. That is, you must have the right attitude, some right habits.

Here are habits necessary for the "good" life.

Good Habits That You Probably Never Thought About

1. Build yourself up (in your mind or out loud) by giving yourself credit for any accomplishment.

2. Warmly accept honest compliments without embarrassment. (Isn't it strange how often the truth hurts a little, even when it's positive?)

3. Be firmly demanding rather than nagging, bitching, or complaining.

4. Help others only when you'd like to and they want you to. Don't sacrifice—ever!

5. Realize that you can always do *something* to change things for the better.

6. Take the occasional calculated risk that might make you feel better. Success is making courageous efforts. Results depend on luck.

7. Take care of yourself first. Satisfied people have more to share.

8. Set reasonable goals. Perfection is a cruel hoax.

9. If you crave magic, look to yourself. Others (doctors, ministers, politicians, authors) possess only the magic you give them.

10. Concentrate on the here and now, rather than on the past or future.

11. Get started right now by giving yourself credit.

BRIEF THERAPY MESSAGE #17
Build self-respect by acting as if you are someone worth knowing.

If you feel you don't have enough self-respect, you share certain habits with many other people. Almost universal are conversations with yourself in which you "let yourself have it": bad names, insults, complaints and criticisms; thinking things like "What is *wrong* with you?" or "There you go again!"

Insults. You can only make yourself feel worse with them. Some people address themselves by name—for others it's just "I" or "you." The result is always the same. If you think, "I'm not good enough," you feel worse.

Why do people insult themselves? The philosophy seems to be: better to criticize or to fail myself rather than risk the greater pain of rejection by others. Putting yourself down can be safe and familiar. But loss of self-respect is a hell of a price!

If you've been listing your shortcomings while reading this book, maybe it's just our subject that makes you feel self-conscious. But we rather doubt that! If you don't have as much self-respect as you'd like, you probably average far more self-insults than self-compliments no matter what you happen to be doing.

Want to find out how much self-respect you really have?

The "What Do I Really Think of Myself?" Exercise

Take a piece of paper and make two lists: your good qualities and your shortcomings, in separate columns. Under each column write down the compliments and insults you give yourself. You will score yourself later on.

We don't know what's on your list, of course, but here's an example:

Good Qualities	*Shortcomings*
sensitive	irritable
warm	hostile
loving	complaining
intelligent	narrow-minded
friendly	withdrawn
capable	helpless
enthusiastic	bored

After you make your list of your personal qualities, make lists of what you do to tell yourself about these qualities. Like this:

Compliments (warm, positive, flattering)	*Insults (hostile, negative, vicious)*
"You did that well"	"You messed that up"
"You are pretty sharp"	"You are really stupid"
"You are doing better"	"You are getting worse"

Write down how many compliments and insults you give yourself during the very first fifteen minutes you spend while you are not reading this book.

How many times you compliment yourself is quite important. The people who are successful—satisfied, loved—compliment themselves quite regularly. People who are frustrated, disgusted, lonely criticize themselves regularly.

To get a sharp focus on your own life, to get control, you need to have self-respect. And to get self-respect, you need to *act as if you already have it.*

Of course, if you feel that you aren't "good enough," you will not try new plans in the first place. If you say more bad things than good to yourself, you will not feel like trying anything. You'll feel defeated before you even start trying to help yourself out of your life trap. But why not "fly"?

So, if in Hour 1 you found you didn't feel the self-respect you want, begin to treat yourself better by complimenting yourself more. Use the good qualities that you do have to give yourself credit for what you do right!

And remember: A compliment is a *compliment.* Don't be halfhearted about it. If you think to yourself, "You didn't mess that up too bad," then that's not nearly as good as "You did that well."

Seek and reward improvement. Don't wait for perfection. Death comes before that!

The experimental-psychology theorists say that when learning is based only on punishment, it is less effective for changing complex behaviors than the use of rewards.

Or, to put it another way, "you can catch more flies with a drop of honey than with a gallon of vinegar."

So do start using compliments. Use your list of good qualities and go to the mirror. Get used to telling yourself what's good about you. Try to give yourself more compliments than criticisms. You will have an opportunity to score yourself at the end of the fifteen minutes.

Give yourself some credit.

Don't panic! Pride is *not* a sin! Putting yourself up is *not* putting others down!

Why not try it? You won't get spoiled! Besides, you deserve it.

O.K., now take that fifteen-minute break.

Now that you've had your break, score yourself.

Give yourself 1 point for every compliment.

If you gave yourself more compliments than insults, give yourself an additional point for every extra compliment.

For example, Helen wrote:

Compliments	*Insults*
1. I'm bright	1. I'm sloppy
2. I'm sensitive	2. I'm overweight
3. I'm warm and loving	3. I'm short-tempered
4. I'm assertive	4. I'm too critical (!!)
5. I'm energetic	
6. I'm good at my work	

Helen gave herself 6 for her 6 compliments and 2 extra for having two more compliments than insults. Her score was 8.

Now take the list of compliments and insults you gave yourself. If you didn't give yourself any compliments, stop reading, and do the exercise again and again until you do!

If you scored 8 or above, you show yourself the love and respect you need to feel worthwhile. Maybe this is the beginning of a new way of treating yourself. Take a five-minute break and celebrate.

If you scored below 8, you insult yourself to a point where you feel frustrated and disgusted very often. Fortunately, you can change this by practice:

Go to a mirror and say three complimentary things to yourself. Utter no insults! Talk loudly and clearly, looking directly at yourself without laughing or looking away. Practice this regularly. You're worth it.

In this exercise you worked on the first of the "Good Habits."—as well as the fifth, the sixth, the seventh, the eighth, the ninth, and the tenth.

Fine! The others (second, third, and fourth) require you to change how you deal with other people. Try them —you'll like it! Here's how:

The First Small Steps to the Good Life

Learning anything new always has to start with the first small steps. For any new behavior, it's the same. Ask yourself: How did I learn to read, to write, to sew, to speak French or Spanish, to swim, to ski, to dance, to sing—or to add in any way to my repertoire of behavior? Any new way of acting, anything you want to add to what you already know, must be learned. You experiment with the new behavior. Try it out—artificially, awkwardly, at first. The best way, as we said before, is by *faking it* at first.

By faking it, risking it, you can begin anything. You take the chance that you might not have immediate and complete success. But faking the first small steps is the *only* way to start.

Behave as if you were the person you would like to become.

Whatever you want to be, start being it: more assertive, more confident, less talkative, warmer, calmer, more open, less clinging, less frightened, more reserved, more comfortable with your anger, more independent.

Whatever you want to be, start it now. Try the new behavior on for size. Start the first small steps.

Maybe you're thinking:

'But that's not *authentic!*" "That's being *hypocritical!*" "But it's *dishonest.*" "It just wouldn't be *real.*" "It *wouldn't be me!*"

And a thousand other ridiculous objections.

Hypocrisy, huh?

Ask yourself again: How do I learn anything?

Why are you thrashing around in the water? Because you don't know how to swim!

Your native tongue is English; what are you trying to prove with your awkward, gross "*comment allez-vous?*" or "*¿Como esta usted?*"

Is it hypocrisy to learn to speak or swim? Dishonesty to learn something new?

Not hypocritical at all, you see. To behave "artificially" to impress or fool *others* while wishing you were doing something else exhausts and demeans you. *That* indeed is dishonesty. But to behave artificially—yes, even awkwardly or grossly—toward your own self, temporarily and in order to become the way *you* want to become—that's the sole process for learning anything new. (If you want to succeed, that is.)

If you want to change what you *are,* change what you *do.* You are what you are for damn good reasons. Your genes and your life experiences have shaped you to behave, think, and feel as you do. Neither you nor we can change your genes or your past. We *would* like to help you change your present and your future. That's what this is all about.

Now is the time and place to start. Sure, in the first small steps you *are* taking the chance that you might not succeed completely when you begin. But risking it, faking it, is where you start to learn.

Perhaps you want your spouse to be more openly loving, more physical, more sensuous. But you're not a demanding person. You're warm, caring, loving, fairly demonstrative. You're comfortable showing your caring. You've hinted at what you'd like, but to no avail.

To ask, or even demand, more concrete loving would be stilted and artificial. Maybe other people can demand the loving they deserve, but it's just not *you* to ask for what's yours. It's not your style. So, if you asked, it wouldn't it be too damn likely to yield a beautiful, spontaneous gesture from your partner.

You may wait forever for that beautiful moment! Go see a movie and settle for vicarious satisfaction. Read a good love story. That's a neat escape. But it won't get you what you want.

Or you can risk it!

Ask, demand, negotiate. Take his or her hand and stroke your face with it. Take his or her arms and wrap them around you. Warmly show how much you appreciate their efforts. Artificially at first, but soon both of you will get better. The gestures will become smoother, the effect more satisfying, the behavior more spontaneous and beautiful. Suddenly you are no longer passive and frustrated. You have changed.

We see this happen all the time.

If you expect instant perfection, you cannot learn anything. By taking the first small steps, you can change. We insist again: You have to fake it and risk it to begin.

"But First I Want to Understand Myself Better"

'But why am I this way?" you may ask. If you want to know, you should see a good therapist and spend the extensive amount of time and money necessary to understand yourself and your past thoroughly.

Then—when you are comfortable that you have achieved insight into your past life and its greater or lesser dissatisfactions—then what?

You can cry about it. You can berate yourself for your past actions. You may label yourself "coward," or "failure," or "lazy." You may blame your parents, or brother or sister, or the Depression, or the War. You may have "worked it through" (that is: You've come to terms with your past). As a result of a productive, prolonged, insight-oriented therapy, you may regret some things, take pride or pleasure in others. Maybe then you will be ready to proceed with your life. Maybe.

Yes, but how? In the same old ways? Or do you wish for something more? You're at the same place—just where you were before your prolonged insight therapy.

Yes, you "understand." But you haven't necessarily changed. It isn't even likely. You may simply have achieved remarkable insight into your continuing unsatisfying behavior.

If you want to change how you are, with (or despite?) your self-understanding, you still must decide in what ways you would like to live differently, and you must practice these ways.

In this brief treatment, we've no time to trace your background and explain why you have become the way you are. We can't afford that luxury in this rapid approach to a more satisfying life.

The achievement of self-understanding may even be putting the cart before the horse.

How come? We know people find self-understanding easier *after* they've changed. Once you are free to behave in new, more satisfying ways, you can much more objectively examine the roots of old habits.

And here's something else we've learned that can save you a lot of time and money: Exploring one's life in order to feel better or more satisfied often is just a convenient excuse to *avoid* change: A copout.

How many people do you know who have been in

therapy for years, yet appear to have changed very little, except that they've aged? They remain uncomfortable, dissatisfied, depressed, weak and hurting. And seem dependent upon therapy. They feel they must continue therapy to exist. They seek solace from therapy—not a better life.

Sure, you can use therapy as evidence of good intentions. Then you can say, "I'm working to improve my life by seeing my therapist regularly!" Fine, but when will you change your life?

Change comes about in the ways we've been telling you.

"*But I Want to Feel Better First*"

Go ahead: Take some tranquilizers, alcohol, or other drug. Or just stay the same and try to take it easy. Get someone to sympathize with your pain and truly feel sorry for you. Isn't it terrible? If only you didn't feel so bad! At least you can have lots of self-pity. It's one way to spend your time.

You can practice saying "If only . . ." Or always be on the verge of giving up. Or hold on to the hope that someday it might all be better.

You can be one of those who watch people and life slowly pass them by and drift away.

If you don't want your life like that, change it. Begin doing what you couldn't do because you were too depressed, hopeless, sad or unloved. Begin now.

As we've said: People who can't change because of the way they feel have good reasons. Their problems bring them benefits. If you don't "feel well," people can't expect much from you. Now ask yourself: Can I give up that safety? You have to if you want to change.

The problems in your life that make you feel bad need to be changed before you can feel better. By taking those first small steps, you can manage it. We've seen it done time after time after time.

"But I Can't Change My Habits"

Habit does make change difficult—even if you weren't afraid of the consequences; even if your friends and relatives didn't resist your changes; even if your changes gave rewarding results, you would still find yourself slipping into the well-traveled grooves of habit: backsliding into your old, "honest" behavior. The comfort and familiarity of habits make it hard to see that how you behave is in fact solely your choice. It's easy to continue your habits and never think about your needs or your self-respect.

Or you can change. Easy, unthinking, automatic, comfortable, but unsatisfying habits—or new, initially artificial, awkward, premeditated behaviors. It's up to you to choose.

You may perfect a new behavior only to discover that it has become a bad habit. And then you might have to change again. So ask yourself: Can I give up my habits and think about what I do?

The Worst Is Over

When you have had enough of the "But I . . ." roadblocks, when you really want to begin, that's when to take the first small steps.

BRIEF THERAPY MESSAGE #18
Take the first small steps and the worst is over.

So choose a small, yet distinct behavior that would move you toward your goal. Pick something that's very likely to succeed—something you can accomplish immediately. Something you can stop any time. Do something that's unlikely to harm you significantly. If you start learning Spanish, you're not committing yourself to take an interpreter's job at the United Nations.

The impotent man fears his first mild success at sexual intercourse; he views it as an obligation to be a stud from then on. The anorgastic (frigid) woman fears her first orgasm will lead to insatiable nymphomania. Have no fear; if you can reverse your failures, you can certainly control your successes.

For example, let's refer back to the passive, retiring person mentioned earlier. He never demands, never intrudes . . . may complain, but never asks for anything outright. Goes along with the crowd. Acquiesces. He is a doormat, with a hungry, humiliated soul.

What can he do to change? Should he run for the Senate? Become a public figure. Unwise. Unnecessary.

But—

He might raise his hand in class and ask a question. He might write a letter to the editor of a newspaper. He might go to his boss with a constructive suggestion. He can *perform* any small but concrete act that contradicts his old, self-effacing manner. Immediately, he'd get more satisfaction and self-respect out of his life!

To make these first small steps succeed, use the following techniques to make them easier.

Call for Reinforcements

BRIEF THERAPY MESSAGE #19
Reward yourself for every effort that you make in the desired direction.

Hopefuly, change will be its own reward. But, damn it, any one with the guts to risk changing deserves encouragement. Many people hire therapists for that purpose. We recommend you reward yourself for your effort.

Allow yourself a favorite luxury for each step you take: an afternoon off, a splurge purchase, a massage, dinner out, sex at noon. It's your effort, your reward, your choice!

People give rewards to children, animals, athletes, musicians, artists—anyone who performs well. It's all part of training. But many people don't know how to reward themselves.

It's difficult to change habits if you don't give yourself reason to bother; reward yourself well, and change will be easier for you.

Emphasize the Positive

Avoid self-criticism. Whatever you do that you're proud of and that satisfies you, *do it more often.*

Fill up your time with positive behavior; squeeze out the negative.

We find this far more productive than "witch hunting" for personal defects. Remember, we're after increased self-regard. Putting yourself down or being put down may produce apparently virtuous self-discipline. But that won't help.

Criticism, of course, can make you aware of self-defeating behavior. More often, though, it is used to avoid change. If you feel bad enough (guilty, ashamed, etc.) about whatever you are doing, you can continue doing it. The guilt or criticism becomes the penalty you pay to continue the destructive behavior—excessive drinking, smoking, procrastination, overeating, wife beating, nose picking, and so forth—so long as you punish yourself sufficiently.

But if you ride your bicycle instead of watching a soap opera while nibbling on a "munchie," you're on the move toward your goal of reduced weight, better physical condition, more fresh air, while placing yourself in far better position to expand relationships.

Of course, you can watch the soap opera, eat some cookies, and wind up where you started out, just by berating yourself. You might "put the icing on the cake," so to speak, by using your spouse, giving him plenty of opportunities to attack you—thus providing him with an interesting evening of entertainment and relaxation.

There is little to be gained by frequent self-criticism. We have often encouraged, or, more accurately, dared, many patients to continue their overeating, excessive drinking, etc.—but to enjoy it! Their shame and guilt obviously did not slow down their self-destructive habits; they might as well have enjoyed them. Before long, they not only stopped the habits, but learned that giving up self-criticism was necessary to make their changes begin to happen.

Remember: You must begin by getting self-respect to get in control of your life.

Get All the Free Help You Can

BRIEF THERAPY MESSAGE #20
Contract with those around you to encourage you (by praise, attention, hugs, kisses—whatever turns you on).

Tell those who are close to you what behavior you are going to change. Ask for their encouragement and help. They might like the change you've planned. Or, they may prefer you the way you are. But don't keep the planned change to yourself if you can get help—free help, from friends, relatives, neighbors, anyone who will give it to you.

What to Do When You Can't Get Anywhere by Doing What You're Doing

What do you do when you've tried everything you can think of and still aren't getting anywhere? The techniques already covered in this book will help you make almost any change you want. One last method will take care of the rest. It's remarkably useful.

BRIEF THERAPY MESSAGE #21
Make all your behaviors *your choice.*

Suppose you want to assert yourself, or stop bitching, or be more sensitive. But you aren't getting anywhere. Even with help from those around you, with rewards to yourself, you still can't succeed. It doesn't happen often, but if it does, here is what to do.

Try something different—vacations, moving, different people, different anything. When you're absolutely stuck, and only after you have used all the other methods, try something different. Often you can't tell in advance what will work best. So, in the interest of improving, experiment.

If you still have an uncomfortable symptom you can't get rid of, try to produce it deliberately. This will increase your control over your behavior and help eliminate the problem.

A brilliant hypnotist and innovator in Brief Therapy determined the actual sleep time and specific hours when insomniacs were convinced they actually slept—for example, four hours per night, generally between 1 and 5 A.M. He then instructed them not to go to bed until 1 A.M., to set their clocks for 5 A.M., and to get up immediately, regardless of how sleepy they might be. Not many nights would pass before sleep improved tremendously. (Or else the directions would be ignored, which demonstrated the patients' desire to retain their insomnia.)

We have successfully treated a number of men suffering from impotence and premature ejaculation by instructing them and their partners to enjoy themselves for several weeks with any and every form of foreplay, but not to indulge in actual intercourse until after their next session, two to three weeks thence. We have been delighted by how successfully we have been disobeyed. The couples return, sheepishly reporting that after a number of nights the product of their efforts appeared so sturdy and dependable that they could no longer resist the enjoyment they had longed for for *so long*.

Others—afraid of "losing control," "going crazy," or "panicking" in new situations—have been encouraged to stop resisting and to, in fact "panic," " go crazy" or in effect bring about the very disruption they feared, with the guarantee that we would hospitalize them if necessary—if they were "successful" and the catastrophe indeed happened.

Symptoms, like enemies, become much less of a threat once they belong to *you* and are under *your* control to do with as *you* will, rather than remaining foreign adversaries, lurking to attack.

Well, we certainly seem to be asking a great deal of you. But you're worth it!

Now move on to Hour 4, where we'll deal with precise steps to get others to help improve your life.

The Fourth Hour:
Getting Others to Help You

Frequently people say to us, "There's somebody I'd like to get closer to, but I just don't know how."

Intimacy. Arranging it can be difficult.

When you are close to someone, you get help with your basic needs. You can't do it all by yourself. Having another person makes love, security, self-respect, fun, and all other good things so much easier to get.

As psychiatrists we hear all sorts of reasons why people want love and intimacy. Most common are these three:

1. Intimacy relieves the incredible loneliness of being close to no one.

2. Intimacy makes a fair trade of love for love and helps fulfill other basic human needs.

3. Intimacy feels good.

Part of intimacy is sharing some of what another person feels. Often, just showing that you care about what they feel is enough to have them want to share with you. Sensitivity is pretty easy to learn. Showing what you feel isn't too hard either.

Then why isn't everybody intimate? Why isn't the whole world madly in love?

Simple. Being in love is risky business.

Here's why:

1. You might offer love or friendship to another, and they might be offended (thinking it was only a sexual advance, etc.). Or, even worse, they might not be interested ("rejection," "put-down," etc.).

2. They might accept your offer, but then make too many demands on you (marriage, economic support, etc.).

3. They might not love you forever.

Can you take those kinds of risks?

It all depends on the belief you have in yourself. Being rejected at the beginning or end of a relationship hurts bad, yes. But—

If you know you're a fine, worthwhile person, that the world is lucky you exist, then you know you will love and be loved throughout your life.

A rejection does not mean *you* are defective.

If you see every personal contact as a test of your self-worth, then you have too much to lose when relating to others. My God—then your self-worth depends on the other person! With every meeting, you rest your self-worth on how the other rates you. That makes life not only too risky, but too exhausting.

Know your beauty and each meeting becomes an opportunity to share with others. If rejected, be saddened by lost opportunity, *not* lost self-worth!

Now, how about the fear of excessive demands that an intimate may make on you?

You can say "no" to anything in a relationship if you know your worth. You can't be devoured if you know you will survive their anger, even their rejection.

It all seems to revolve around self-respect, doesn't it?

So again, ask yourself: Can I take the risks? Be sure, please, because you're about to learn techniques that just might get you in much deeper than you want.

Find out whether you can "take it" by taking . . .

The "Is It Really Worth the Trouble?" Exercise

Ask yourself: Do I want to take the chance of getting close to ______ [Fill in the name of someone you'd like to be closer to], even though they may . . .

	Yes	*No*
reject my advance?	☐	☐
accept, but demand more than I want to give?	☐	☐
not love me for ever and ever?	☐	☐

If you can't answer "yes" to all these questions, then don't bother with intimacy. For you, it just isn't worth the trouble. Sorry, but getting love takes effort. You have to do something to get it. You have to feel worthwhile, or risk behaving as if you are until you feel it.

If you can answer "yes" to the questions, then try the following techniques.

Don't worry if you're not completely satisfied with intimacy. You can always go back to loneliness. There's real safety in loneliness. No one will bother you, demand anything from you, hurt you, or disappoint you. Right?

(You will, of course, be all alone.)

If you want to take the chance of getting closer, here are a few ways that work:

"I Can't Hear You"

The best place to start is by listening. Not just to words, but to feelings, too. Remember: Sensitivity can be learned.

Hearing what someone is saying is pretty easy. If you want to improve your listening, try this:

First, listen to what they say. Then ask yourself, "What are they thinking and feeling?" Then repeat to them what you think they were saying.

Easy? Common-sense? Obvious? Of course. Yet, few people go through these steps, even though the results are often dramatic and surprising.

By checking out what you hear, you're telling others that you're listening, that what they say is *important,* that you really *care* about what they think and feel. You may feel a little awkward at first, but give it a try. Even if you're the "quiet type." It's all right to ask questions, make guesses, reach out. Really it is.

Like this:

BETTY: I'm thinking of going to that concert next week.

MIKE: (Thinking to himself, "Does she want to be with *me*?"): Would you like to go with *me*?

BETTY: Well, yes, I'd really like to!
MIKE: I'd like to take you.

The intimate contact has now been made.
Or:

JIM: Did you really have to bring up that fight we had when we were with John and Pat last night?
ELLEN: (Thinking to herself, "He really sounds angry"): Are you sore at me about that, Jim?
JIM: Yes, I *am* angry!
ELLEN: It was careless of me. I was still damned irritated from our fight, but I shouldn't have brought it up then.

The intimate air has now been cleared.

To find intimacy, you need to be sensitive to feelings. You might not hear only things you like. You may find love and affection where you don't expect it. You may find rejection and anger. Being close means not always getting what you want. Loneliness is much safer.

If you want intimacy, then learn how to acquire more sensitivity to what you hear—not only to the words, but the tone, the volume, the mood of other voices. And by asking questions, you can ask others to help you understand them. Which brings us to

BRIEF THERAPY MESSAGE #22
To listen thoroughly, ask a few questions. They're cheap and easy, and will help you understand.

What You See Is What You Get

Can you guess what someone is feeling even without listening to what they say? Of course! You do it all the time, without even thinking about it. Facial expression, tone of voice, body movements—they often speak more clearly and honestly than words. "Non-verbal communication" is the formal term. All it means is communicating without words. Everybody does it. Everybody "listens." But few people get as much out of this kind of listening as they might. Movements communicate a lot about human relationships.

Getting more sensitive to non-verbal (eye) communication is as easy as (ear) listening. Look at a person, then ask yourself, "What is he [or she] saying?" Then check it out by asking. Be sure to notice details. Here's what to look for:

FACIAL EXPRESSION

What do you see? Feelings of sadness, in a quiet, pained look? Or fear, with wide-eyed and tense appearance? Or anger and frustration, with a flat expression or a hostile glance? Or love, affection that is warm smiles and laughter?

Ask yourself. Then ask the other person. But remember: You won't see if you don't look!

Are there feelings they can't or won't put into words? Feelings they might not even be thinking about? Ask yourself, then ask them. Don't assume you know. Think to ask.

Eyes, face wrinkles, mouth—there really aren't any obscure meanings. Look and ask yourself, "How does their facial expression make me feel? What might they be feeling?" Then ask them to find out.

BREATHING AND TONE OF VOICE

These are important, but often people overlook them. Tone of voice is hard to miss. But ask yourself: Does it fit what they're saying? If it doesn't, ask why.

Breathing is a definite message, especially the long, drawn-out sigh, like *ohhhhhh!* It may be relaxation. More often, it's anger and frustration. A sudden gasp means fear or surprise; a long breath in and a long breath out with open mouth, sadness and resignation; a loud breath out, with pursed lips, anger.

You'll notice it in conversations:

> BOB: Wouldn't you like to go to the game with me next weekend?
>
> SALLY: Ohhhhh, yeah, I guess so.

Bob should have understood the message that Sally did not want to go. Maybe she didn't want to take the effort to say "no." Or maybe she was afraid to be honest. Her sigh told him, but he didn't (or wouldn't) hear it, and was afraid to ask.

BODY MOVEMENTS

Messages people give with their bodies say many things. How physically close two people are tells something about their relationship. On the other hand, someone with tightly crossed arms or legs may be saying, "Don't get too close to me." The varieties of body messages are so wide that many books have been written listing them. But you can understand them easily by looking and asking yourself what they are saying with their body. Ask yourself, "How do they feel?" Then ask them to find out for sure.

Making sense out of non-verbal communication involves much initial guessing, so be sure to check and ask, "Is this how you feel?" or "Do you feel like this?" The more you do it, the better you'll get. Being a better friend or lover takes sensitivity. Learn to recognize non-verbal communication, because

BRIEF THERAPY MESSAGE #23
Maybe it's corny, but it's true: "It's not what they say, it's how they say it."

So use your eyes, your ears, and your guts to guess what the other feels. Share this understanding out loud, with feeling. Get feedback to correct your guesses, until the other knows you truly understand.

Avoid advice or, worse, reassurance: "There, there now . . . everything will be all right," "Why don't you . . ." These block understanding. They prevent intimacy.

The empathic approach is powerful! Sharing any profound feeling with another during a fight . . . while making love . . . at work meeting a tough deadline . . . while playing an exciting game . . . brings you closer, because

BRIEF THERAPY MESSAGE #24
Shared emotions are the bridges between people.

How to Hassle for Fun and Profit

Now you know how to be more sensitive to another person's feelings; how to show loving feelings to someone you care about. But really, to show love you've also got to show anger. Holding back irritation, frustration, aggravation will make you hold back love, too.

We find that most people need practice with sharing anger, because we've all been trained to hold it back. "Don't start a fight!" "Don't lose your temper!" That's what we hear.

Anger can indeed damage loved ones, friends, property, even lives. So customs, child-rearing practices, religious traditions, and laws enforce the standard "Don't show your anger."

But many people have learned these cultural lessons too well. They rarely even recognize their own anger. And yet, unexpressed anger, next to loneliness, probably keeps more therapists, physicians, hospitals, pharmaceutical houses, and distilleries in business than any other behavior.

Anger is part of being human, a fundamental part of a person's "coping capacity." Anger energizes our bodies, mobilizes us when we feel threatened. Properly used, good, honest *loving, caring anger* can improve your life, as well as the lives of those close to you. Bottle it up and either your body or your mind will break down, sooner or later.

You want what you want. Your spouse, lover, friend, boss, fellow worker—they all want what they want. You are different people. It would be impossible always to agree. Disagreeing, hassling, fighting—constructively—are often necessary ways of bargaining. Hence:

BRIEF THERAPY MESSAGE #25
Expressing anger openly, honestly, with words and feelings, to defend your self-respect or the well-being of those for whom you care, is a truly loving act.

How good are you at this? Here's how to find out.

The "True Friend" Exercise

A. *When did I last get angry?*
B. *When did I last get angry at the person I love the most?*
C. *Did I tell them?*
D. *. . . with honest emotion?*
E. *. . . directly?*

If you answered A and B in terms of days or a few weeks, if you answered "yes" to C, D, and E, then you have a solid relationship, self-respect, respect for them, love, and true courage. If A and B were answered in terms of years, either you swallow a great deal of crap from others or you are incredibly insensitive to the world around you, and/or you hide your cowardice and low self-respect behind a veneer of "niceness."

If A and B were recent but C was "no," you likely fear that your relationship is so fragile that honesty might destroy it. If D was "no," you likely fear the same, or your own feelings. If only E was "no," not bad—but there's room for improvement.

The ability to express anger is most important in the really close relationships (i.e., couples). We've all met couples who insist they never fight. Usually they're even proud of it, yet one or both must feel deprived or enslaved. Most of the couples we see who are in trouble are unable to fight productively.

Edward Albee's magnificent play *Who's Afraid of Virginia Woolf?* depicts a free-swinging, destructive, relationship style. You can tell they care deeply about each other —they're always fighting. Loving would be too risky. Too much warmth would breed intimacy. Such intimacy, so cherished, would be too painful to lose. This sort of fighting is destructive and useless.

You need to know how to hassle well in many situations. But hassling with a partner in a couple relationship is the most demanding. Learn how to do it right.

BRIEF THERAPY MESSAGE #26

In a successful argument, both parties win if they

do it right! Try to *defeat* the other in battles and you will lose the relationship.

Doing it right involves learning the process of negotiation and bargaining. As always: selfishly, responsibly, and self-respectfully.

But first a basic decision, please. Do you simply want to inflict pain and destruction, to extract vengeance for suffered injustice? Do you want a clear victor declared at the conclusion of the battle?

Yes ☐ No ☐

If you checked "No" and want more from your relationships than you've been getting up to now, we have some suggestions to make any hassle more productive. To show how to use them, we'll tell you about Steve and Nancy.* They had spent five years fighting unproductively, and were about to divorce.

The R & R (Rusk & Read) Rules for Creative Combat

1. *Bring out discomfort quickly.*

As soon as you sense discomfort in the relationship, share your concern, even if the cause remains uncertain. Don't save up resentment. That's not doing anybody a

* Learning how to hassle with someone you're close to will make you stronger in all relationships.

favor (except maybe the "headache and upset-stomach relief" manufacturers).

Steve and Nancy used to do it this way: If she felt he wasn't talking to her enough on Monday, she would wait till Friday, allowing the anger to build, documenting her case . . . then *wham!* Like this:

"Steve, you *never* talk to me! You're *always* working, watching TV, or playing tennis, but you *always* want your meals on time! You've *made* me into a prostitute/housekeeper!" And so on and on and on.

By saying something about her beef on Monday, she wasn't nearly so angry: "Steve, I'm feeling distant from you today, and I don't know why. Let's talk about it, O.K.?"

2. *Contract for mutual change* (tell the partner what you want).

What does your partner do that you don't like? What would you prefer? What would you do in return?

The worst way to fight is to bitch and complain without offering a plan for change.

Like: He comes home at a different time each night and expects supper ready and tasty. You'd like him to call just before he leaves the office, and to appreciate the effort and creativity involved in meal preparation.

Or: You'd like her to build you up once in a while instead of slicing you up in front of company.

Decide what change you'd most appreciate and ask for that. Make it something that can be done starting this week. Ask what change in your behavior your partner wants in exchange. This way, you both assume the risk of changes, and you both reward the other.

3. *Give and demand feedback.*

Is what you're saying really what they're hearing? Is what they're saying really what you're hearing?

How can you both know for certain? Are you perhaps just talking (yelling, screaming) to score points before a real or imagined audience? Are you simply stomping on your victim? Is that what you really want to do? Then go on blindly. What the hell is the difference anyway?

Remember Nancy's line from our example: "Steve, you *never* talk to me." What could Steve do? He could curse. Or retaliate. Or give an itemized account of the times he *had* talked, starting with the time when he asked her for their first date to that very morning, when he asked her to pass the butter.

But *if* you want to fight constructively, make sure you understand what they really mean by what they're saying. And make sure that they understand you, too.

Steve could repeat word for word whatever Nancy said in their arguments. But when he asked her whether she seriously meant that he *never* talked to her, he was surprised at her answer. She told him tearfully that she meant she was afraid he was going to leave her.

Surprises of such magnitude are common, so the more frequent the feedback, the better you'll understand yourself and the other.

4. *Stick to the present.*

Historical anecdotes or amateur fortunetelling, as in "Remember when you said I wasn't any good in bed?" and "You'll never change, you'll always put the children first." are obstructive maneuvers. Fight about the present, and keep off the past and future. (Actually, this is part of Rule No. 2, since negotiating works best on what you want changed *now*.)

5. *Be explicitly empathic.*

This is most difficult when you're angry, of course. If you can pull it off, you move into the expert category. From time to time as you give and receive feedback, try to put yourself in the partner's place. How would it feel to be in the other person's shoes and to be relating to you? Would you risk reversing roles in the argument? (Take a chance: Play your partner's role and let him/her play you for five minutes.) If nothing else, you should get a good laugh out of putting some distance between yourself and your stake in the situation.

6. *Allow enough time to finish the fight.*

Walking out in mid-argument is destructive violence. If you must stop because you're about to slug him/her, or Mother Nature is calling, or the telephone is ringing, then stop temporarily. But make sure to schedule when you'll continue.

Avoid quick jabs as you leave in the morning, such as Steve would use: "If you call that 'being together' at breakfast, I'd rather you'd slept in!" (Exits, slamming door.)

These parting shots leave lingering destructive fallout behind. If you're going to fight, then make sure you *fight*. Arrange several hours, to be interrupted only by mutually agreed-upon recesses.

Remember, the following do not constitute justifiable reasons to stop:

a) crying

b) yelling
c) a TV special is starting
d) "the kids will know we're fighting"
e) one of you is getting a headache.

7. *No audiences! No grandstanding!*

A good fight is a creative partnership session to work something out for mutual benefit. Open arenas encourage playing to the crowd, taking sides, pyrotechnics, and keeping score—none of which helps in the least.

Audiences have their place at sporting events, plays, and politics. They don't belong in intimate relationships. To improve your satisfaction from your interaction with that certain someone, avoid an audience. Your battles should be open, so they had best be private.

8. *No labels! No name-calling!*

Remember your goal: to change how you behave toward each other. Pigeonholing, condemning, insulting—all such maneuvers block progress toward change.

Steve and Nancy had come up with many accurate and vicious insults, and their fights were mainly name-calling:

"You're just like your mother."
"You're a selfish bastard."
"You're a nagging bitch."
"You're filth."

And so on . . .

Not productive, and easy to avoid—*if* you care for the other person.

9. *No physical violence, but do show your feelings!*

Physical abuse makes a satisfying, constructive end to any hassle almost impossible. On the other hand, a fight without sharing honest feelings, even yelling, is just a pallid mockery of the real thing.

Steve and Nancy were out to dinner. He was angry, but said calmly while buttering his bread, "Darling, making fun of my impotence won't help matters . . ." He was angry because she had acted cold and unfeeling. Making his point without emotion was so dishonest that he made as little impact at dinner as he had in bed the previous evening.

10. *Silence is vicious.*

Using silence is the same as walking out of an argument. It will destroy a relationship when used consistently. Avoid it.

11. *If necessary, agree to disagree.*

Occasionally you'll reach an impasse. So what? If you disagree, clarify the feedback. Repeat what you understand your partner to be saying, and have the other show you he/she knows what you're saying. Agree on understanding each other, but agree to disagree.

She feels that your mutual pal Sam is a bore. You feel he's brilliant. Two thousand hours of discussion and a nationwide opinion poll won't necessarily change your minds. Nor will dragging out that argument bring the two of you together. It's time to agree to disagree, and to go on.

12. *Your feelings and your actions are your responsibility.*

As you argue, remember that what you think, what

you feel, what you say, what you do—all belong to you. You have a right to your feelings, you have a right to speak your piece. *But,* you can't make anyone else responsible.

He or she doesn't *make* you angry, doesn't *make* you drink, doesn't *make* you think ill of yourself. Oh, you might react in these ways to what the other person does or says. That's your choice. But efforts to place responsibility for your thoughts, feelings, or actions on others lead to endless accusations and recriminations.

This Is Irresponsibility

> When you criticize me *you* make me so angry that *I have to* have a drink [cigarette, something to eat]. You're killing me!

This Is Courage

> When you criticize I get angry. I handle my anger by drinking [smoking, eating]. I'm hurting myself.

Instead of being trapped, you suddenly are free to choose.

Creative Combat—the Follow-Through

Pay close attention to the following principles. They're necessary to assure long-term payoffs from creative combat.

BRIEF THERAPY MESSAGE #27
Emphasize the positive.

You've had the combat. You've contracted for mutual changes. Your partner is obviously trying to make the changes you've asked for—or even demanded. But habits are powerful. Your partner is not perfect (are you?). He/she is going to slip back to the old ways from time to time.

What to do?

Ignore the backsliding so long as you see positive efforts. Reward these efforts. Demonstrate your appreciation by word and deed. If you both *keep trying* the change and keep rewarding each other for fine efforts and ignore the occasional slips, you're well on your way!

Some intimates are so afraid of disappointment and so afraid to hope that they latch on to the slips, embrace the failures, clutch at the evidence of old behavior that so bothered them in the past. They emphasize the negatives and ignore efforts at change.

Their game is: "Prove you're a changed person and I'll relax and enjoy you. If I reward your efforts too soon, you'll just disappoint me. I'll feel foolish and hurt all the more for having hoped and tried."

These people have made an important and unfortunate choice. They'll never achieve greater satisfaction. But at least they won't feel the acute pain that occurs when one dares to try and hope. We understand their fear. We regret their choice.

What if your partner refuses to engage in creative combat? What if no real efforts at cooperative change occur? Then remember:

BRIEF THERAPY MESSAGE #28
Use your leverage.

Ask yourself:

How much do I value my self-respect? Do I have as much right to satisfy my needs as anyone on earth?

Now your responses to the exercises and messages from Hour 1 become pivotal.

It's so easy to spot people who choose to remain victims: They whine and complain; they bitch and nag; they moan. They shake, look defeated, walk slump-shouldered, lack energy, are easily irritated, catch colds easily, miss work or school, suffer constantly from an endless variety of non-critical infirmities.

Why?

Because they will not use the leverage they have with others.

First, you must *ask* for what you want.

Why? Because loving you does not necesarily mean being able to read your mind.

And if the asking doesn't work?

Demand! Demanding (as opposed to nagging, bitching, and complaining) implies a creatively selected, escalating sequence of sanctions that you will bring to bear until your needs are met.

Should you be willing to negotiate, compromise, discuss alternatives? Of course! Ultimatums must absolutely be saved as a last resort.

Remember: Only the willingness to demand can get you more than you've got. And demands are only bluffs if you are unwilling to impose tactical sanctions. Bluffing will not work for long. You must be willing to use your nuclear weapons ultimately. Otherwise tactical weapons won't work.

You say you'd never use nuclear weapons? Don't be so sure!

Ask yourself: What behavior on his/her part would provoke me to end the relationship (leave the marriage, quit the job, end the friendship)? Will I risk imposing sanctions if he/she might leave (fire, avoid) me in retaliation? Would anything cause me to risk living without that particular relationship?

"Till death do us part," you say? Then you have chosen slavery, or perhaps suicide or homicide. Is that really what you have in mind?

Unless you set limits to the compromise of your needs and your self-respect, you *are* a slave. And the condition of slavery can become so painful that you will eventually attempt escape, through illness, alcohol, drugs, hypochondria, breaking the law, or some other form of invalidism.

If you can't survive without your partner . . . if "peace at any price" is your game . . . if your self-respect and your needs are not worth the hassle, then you've got bad trouble, because you have no leverage. You are doomed to remain forever dissatisfied, envying those who have mastered the methods of successful living.

Nancy the mousy housewife nags, bitches, complains about her "male-fascist-pig" husband. She suffers from recurrent back pain, which makes her life miserable. It also effectively punishes Steve, by adding financial burdens (doctor bills) to his sex-deprived existence.

Steve treats her terribly, she complains. He's never home. He's selfish, unloving. In bed it's "Bim, bam, thank you, ma'am!", with foreplay restricted to a "How about some tonight, honey?"

But . . . but . . . but . . .

Has she ever considered forcefully stating her unsatisfied needs? Has she made demands? Would she be willing to deprive him of things he gets from her and apply direct, up-front sanctions (honest blackmail, if you wish)? Would she stop cooking his special meals? Would she refuse even if her back were fine? Would she take a vacation by herself? Would she not go to all the trouble of searching for the many amenities that he takes for granted? Would she be willing to deprive him and say so, honestly and directly, warning him that unless he changes his behavior she will retaliate? Well, would she?

If nothing else worked, would she leave him permanently to salvage her self-respect and seek satisfaction elsewhere?

Ask yourself. If asking, rewarding the real efforts, and then demanding with appreciation of appropriate leverage all don't work, would you continue to put up with your humiliating dissatisfaction? Are you doing so in some relationship at home, at work, or socially, right now? Are you sure?

Many people, lacking the courage to fight, suffer (with or without complaint) for years. Then, suddenly, they quit the intolerable situation (marriage, job, friendship). But they never even give the other person (s) a chance to work out a solution. They use their ultimate weapon right off and never employ the tactical arsenal to reshape the other person (spouse, boss, friend) to be reasonably responsive to their own needs.

They'd rather run than risk (a fight).

Can't people just get along without having to hassle, to lead a satisfied self-respecting life?

Want the answer straight?

No!

No two people, no situation, can be perfect enough to allow that kind of permanent peace on earth.

In summary: Loving warmth breeds intimacy; occasional loving anger invigorates a relationship. So intimacy is a marvelous but risky business.

BRIEF THERAPY MESSAGE #29

Love does not hold people together. Rather, like a garden of fragile flowers, it takes hard work and nurturing to cultivate love and make it thrive.

Willing to risk it?

The Hours from Now On

Time's up!

If you have used this book as we designed it, you've changed. Great—but be vigilant! The new ways of living that you began in the four hours' reading will require practice to become as automatic as the old habits you gave up. You have changed, but you can drift back to where you were. The Brief Therapy Messages are collected here. Check yourself out regularly.

You can re-read our ideas from time to time, but from here on out, it's really up to *you*.

We have done our best. We know that the ideas, exercises, and approaches to living in this book have helped a great many people in and outside of therapy. We invested our efforts to satisfy your needs and to increase your self-respect. We proudly take full responsibility for the contents.

We wish you the same in your life endeavors.

Good luck!

The Brief Therapy Messages

(WITH SOME FINAL COMMENTS BY THE AUTHORS)

BRIEF THERAPY MESSAGE #1

We want you to love yourself. We want you to take responsibility for your actions. We wish you selfish satisfaction of your needs.

(A philosophy for successful living.)

BRIEF THERAPY MESSAGE #2

You can make yourself be the way *you* want to be!

(The crucial concept of choice and freedom vs. *oppression and invalidism.)*

BRIEF THERAPY MESSAGE #3

If you don't put your needs first—who will?

(A question of priorities.)

BRIEF THERAPY MESSAGE #4

Control involves belief in your freedom to choose. Free-

dom to choose involves the responsibility of choosing. Therefore, freedom, responsibility, and control are inseparable.
(Everything has a price, or, put differently, slaves can be irresponsible.)

BRIEF THERAPY MESSAGE #5

If you don't take care of your needs, you can take care of nothing well.
(Love, like charity, begins at home.)

BRIEF THERAPY MESSAGE #6

Oh, to feel loved just because you exist! That's the best there is!
(Nirvana!)

BRIEF THERAPY MESSAGE #7

Once you recognize your worth, you can spend your time using it rather than having to work at earning it.
(Stop chasing the carrot in front of your nose—it's within your grasp.)

BRIEF THERAPY MESSAGE #8

Make play a high priority and you enrich your entire life.
(Play, like a balanced diet, is essential.)

BRIEF THERAPY MESSAGE #9

Brief therapy is one way of learning how to get back what you may have given up—*quickly!*
(How quickly is up to you.)

BRIEF THERAPY MESSAGE #10

You can make your style work by thinking about your needs more and using habits less.
(Old habits don't work in the electronic age of future shock.)

BRIEF THERAPY MESSAGE #11

If you can't love yourself, you can't love anyone else. *(We agree with all the sages.)*

BRIEF THERAPY MESSAGE #12

Will (does) the behavior satisfy you and increase your self-respect?
(Crucial . . . and only you can decide!)

BRIEF THERAPY MESSAGE #13

"Sick" habits (bad escapes) have their good points, too. *(There are "good" reasons for everything.)*

BRIEF THERAPY MESSAGE #14

Take reasonable risks that may improve need satisfaction and increase self-worth.
("To thine own self be true"—or "Try it, you'll like it.")

BRIEF THERAPY MESSAGE #15

This week *work, play, love* in new ways—ways you may have wished to try but were afraid to risk for fear of embarrassment, rejection, failure.
(Please, *get moving!*)

BRIEF THERAPY MESSAGE #16

To think differently is to think differently, but to behave differently is to *be* different.
(Fake it! Learn it! *Then* master it!)

BRIEF THERAPY MESSAGE #17

Build self-respect by acting as if you are someone worth knowing.
(An excellent point is worth repeating.)

BRIEF THERAPY MESSAGE #18

Take the first small steps and the worst is over.

(A matter of overcoming inertia.)

BRIEF THERAPY MESSAGE #19

Reward yourself for every effort that you make in the desired direction.

(Be your own behavior therapist.)

BRIEF THERAPY MESSAGE #20

Contract with those around you to encourage you (by praise, attention, hugs, kisses—whatever turns you on).

(Advanced behavior therapy.)

BRIEF THERAPY MESSAGE #21

Make all your behavior *your choice.*

(Gives you freedom and self-control but eliminates copouts.)

BRIEF THERAPY MESSAGE #22

To listen thoroughly, ask a few questions. They're cheap and easy, and will help you understand.

(Assumptions are incredibly dangerous.)

BRIEF THERAPY MESSAGE #23

Maybe it's corny, but it's true: "It's not what they say, it's how they say it."

(The medium is the message—McLuhan.)

BRIEF THERAPY MESSAGE #24

Shared emotions are the bridges between people.

(You may have loved a car or a dress, but did it love you?)

BRIEF THERAPY MESSAGE #25

Expressing anger openly, honestly, with words and feelings, to defend your self-respect or the well-being of those for whom you care, is a truly loving act.

(Think of Jesus and the money lenders; Moses returning from the mountain.)

BRIEF THERAPY MESSAGE #26

In a successful argument, both parties win if they do it right! Try to *defeat* the other in battles and you will lose the relationship.

(Turn your arguments into creative combats.)

BRIEF THERAPY MESSAGE #27

Emphasize the positive.

(Platitudes can be important.)

BRIEF THERAPY MESSAGE #28

Use your leverage.

(It takes courage.)

and finally . . .

BRIEF THERAPY MESSAGE #29

Love does not hold people together. Rather, like a garden of fragile flowers, it takes hard work and nurturing to cultivate love and make it thrive.

Scientific Appendix

Note: Numbers in parentheses refer to the Bibliography, starting on p. 112

We recognize that this is an arrogant book. In a time when people insist on "the fastest relief," to offer this book may seem almost outrageous. Certainly, it raises an obvious question: Why hasn't Brief Therapy been thought of before?

Actually, briefness in therapy is not at all new. It may seem new because its popularity in psychotherapy has been intermittent at best. Yet psychoanalysis, the first of the "psychological" psychotherapies, began with Freud's attempts at quick cures. Many of his successful treatments were accomplished in six sessions or less (3, 11). Over the years the theoretical complexity of psychoanalysis increased, and the duration of treatment lengthened. Several years of four to five intensive sessions weekly is now considered the minimum for effective treatment. This trend began to change when Alexander and French in 1946 (1) attempted to revise psychoanalytic therapy comprehensively to fit known, effective, practical techniques, in what they called "Brief Therapy."

Today, most therapy has to be brief. People don't have time for long-term treatment. And there aren't enough therapists to go around. Many therapists have felt this need, and briefer versions of various treatments have been developed. These have been extensively reviewed by Small (19) and Phillips and Wiener (16). The latter authors review a number of controlled studies demonstrating the efficacy of structured Brief Therapy, including comparisons with longer-term approaches. Connecting the practical experience with available theoretical formulations has usually been difficult.*

A dilemma of psychotherapies of all kinds has been to explain effective techniques in terms of formal theory. Theory A may explain why Technique #1 produces a favorable result. But it may not predict the effect of Technique #2 in the same situation; or it may predict a poor outcome when the therapist, the patient, and the patient's family all think the outcome was very good indeed. (The therapist is in an even worse position when he is a member of an association founded on Theory A.)

Theoretical formulations such as Psychoanalysis, Behaviorism, Reality Therapy, Transactional Analysis, Client-Oriented Therapy, etc., are quite helpful to the therapist. They are attempts to understand complex phenomena in terms of the smallest number of premises. When a new observation does not fit the therapy in use, there is a limited number of alternatives. One can revise a portion of the theory to explain the observation; create

* For one attempt, see Rusk (18).

a whole new theoretical formulation; or ignore the observation. This last possibility is all too common. Therapists often will not even admit to using techniques that disagree with accepted theory, regardless of how effective they are in practice (4).

More often, theories get revised. Psychoanalysis, being the oldest of the widely used theories of psychotherapy, has been continually revised, to the point of unworkable complexity. Transactional Analysis, though much newer, is headed the same way.

Measurement is what all psychotherapy really lacks. There are few replicable observations of behavior. Much less is there a rigorous and widely accepted measure of outcome effectiveness. This difficulty has been widely discussed throughout the scientific literature. Kiesler (12) presents a lucid exposition of the problem and some approaches to comparing different therapies, therapists, and patients. Still, there is little agreement on what even as simple a term as "patient improvement" means.

Nevertheless, it is possible to define what most therapists accept as favorable outcomes: relief of symptoms (whatever the patient would like to get rid of: overeating, smoking, anxiety, etc.); revision of the internal economy to reduce symptom occurrence (ego functioning, self-actualization, personality integration, etc.).

Rather than limit ourselves to a single theory, we have borrowed widely from other therapists to use what is most effective in actual practice. As most therapists know, different therapies do not necessarily produce different results. Jerome Frank has advanced compelling arguments to suggest that therapists of different theoretical backgrounds actually use much the same techniques (5).

It may be that there are general principles of psychotherapy which, regardless of the specific patient's problems, are used by every effective therapist. These have been described by Frank, and they are evident in the methods used by therapists to affect their patients (5).

People seek treatment to relieve their discomfort. To accomplish this, the therapist/client interaction must accomplish some *change*—in attitude, feelings, and/or behavior on the part of the client.

The various therapies involve one or more of the following for influencing or changing clients (17):

— a powerful relationship is created
— emotional release is encouraged
— self-awareness (insight) is fostered
— a theoretical rationale is offered
— expectation of change from old to new attitudes, feelings, and behavior is implicitly or explicitly encouraged
— frequent repetition (practice) of revised thinking, feeling, and/or behaving is emphasized
— some contract covering mutual expectations regarding duration, changes, responsibilities, and so forth is implicitly or explicitly negotiated
— hope of distress, relief, or of increased satisfaction (pleasure) is suggested
— a person's ability to choose to be different is explicitly or implicitly suggested

Although we approach our patients from our medical backgrounds, people-influencers can be religious or other counselors—including faith healers, witch doctors, educators, attorneys, jailors, rehabilitation counselors, advertising-media people, salesmen, family, friends, and neighbors. Regardless, all make use of the fundamentals cited above.

Each emphasizes some techniques more than others. Each has its own style, language, expected duration of individual sessions for the entire therapy.

Since there is no concise way to measure effectiveness, we rely on the therapist's and the patient's views of improvement, along with the judgments of those in social contact with the patient. Since we draw from general principles of practical psychotherapy and use a wide variety of techniques, there is not sufficient space to list all of those from whom we have borrowed. Likewise, only a few references to studies of particular techniques will be listed.

We view the patient as an open individual system (interacting with other open systems), to be changed by the interaction of that system with the therapist.

Many therapists have been influenced by these concepts from systems theory, but Bateson, Haley (10), and their associates have best illustrated their practical applications. Phillips's and Wiener's review of systems theory as applied to brief therapy can be found in their excellent book (16).

Consciously and explicitly, we attempt to make use of *every* fundamental of effective therapy. We try to establish as powerful a relationship as possible (10, 5, 8). We use empathy assertively to foster greater awareness and release of feelings (20). We focus on self-awareness, especially regarding current attitudes, feelings, and behavior at home, work, and play, as in Reality Therapy (7). We use a simple transactional framework, as is done in Transactional Analysis (2), involving needs, self-respect, responsibility, and choice in the analytic tradition (21). We borrow heavily from the Behaviorists in our assertive encouragement to focus on specific behavioral goals, to change behavior so as to change one's life.

We see this as far more crucial than insight, or reliving early life experiences which unquestionably have produced current life habits. Without jargon, we can encourage a self-awareness of current life satisfactions, dissatisfactions, and a self-concept that is totally within the grasp of the average layman. Then we utilize the concepts of becoming different by behaving differently (faking it), as well as repetitive practice to consolidate changes (9). We freely ridicule self-destructive behaviors, while maintaining steadfast respect for the potential in each person to rapidly improve his or her life (4). In our face-to-face sessions and in this book, we encourage written assignments to clarify current life assessments and clearer behavioral goal-setting (16). We have found structured inventories very useful for these purposes, and use several regularly in our clinical practice.

We are convinced that, within wide limits, expectation of rapid change (14), explicit contract negotiation (2, 15), emphasis on the present (16, 20), on the positive (1), and on new behavior now (16, 22) can and do produce rapid changes in a wide variety of people.

In each application we vary the techniques to fit the individual and to avoid boredom for ourselves. No exact formula yields what a therapist should do at any moment. Rather, the effort is made to balance and compensate after each exchange to direct the course of therapy toward the therapeutic principles. Therapy today is not an arrow shot from a bow; it is a line drawn from a pen, and it demands constant, fine corrective movements to proceed smoothly.

It may seem peculiar that while so many turn to mystical truths or biochemistry, we should choose to see man as a decision-making problem solver. We too have struggled with this. We believe that self-respect, self-control, and individual responsibility are the most human things about man. Regardless of our existence in worlds we can't see, we do have this one to deal with. Staying a whole person and doing what is yours to do is still possible. Even the identification of biochemical factors in psychiatric "diseases" will not eradicate the problems we face when we are "well." You still have to decide what to do with yourself every day of your life!

We anticipate criticism from our colleagues that we have presumed far too much by writing a book for the layman which expects significant long-term change to be produced rapidly simply by reading a book.

Perhaps they will be correct. The opinions of both colleagues and patients are important. You can help by telling us yours. Ideally, each of you would write us in care of our publisher and inform us as to: every change in your life (good or bad) directly attributable to your reading and using this book; the most useful idea, exercise, or section in the book; the least useful idea, exercise, or section; any additional comments.

We thank you.

Bibliography

1. Alexander, F., and French, T. *Psychoanalytic Therapy*. New York: Ronald Press, 1946.
2. Berne, E. *Principles of Group Treatment*. New York: Oxford University Press, 1964.
3. Breuer, J., and Freud, S. *Studies on Hysteria*. Boston: Beacon Press, 1937.
4. Coleman, J. "Banter as Psychotherapeutic Intervention." *American Journal of Psychoanalysis, 22*, 1962, pp. 69–74.
5. Frank J. *Persuasion and Healing*. Baltimore: Johns Hopkins Press, 1961.
6. Freud, S. "Observations on 'Wild' Psychoanalysis," in the standard edition of the complete psychological works of Sigmund Freud. London: The Hogarth Press, 1957.
7. Glasser, A. *Reality Therapy*. New York: Harper & Row, 1965.
8. Goldstein, A., Heller, K., and Sechrest, L. *Psychotherapy and the Psychology of Behavior Change*. New York: John Wiley & Sons, 1966, pp. 73–145.
9. Goldstein, A. *Psychotherapeutic Attraction*. Academic Press, New York, 1971, pp. 140–149.

10. Haley, J., and Hoffman, L. *Techniques of Family Therapy*. New York: Basic Books, 1967.
11. Jones, E. *The Life and Work of Sigmund Freud*, Vol. II. New York: Basic Books, 1957.
12. Kiesler, D. "Experimental Designs in Psychotherapy Research," *Handbook of Psychotherapy and Behavior Changes*. Bergin, A., and Garfield, S. (Eds.). New York: Wiley, 1971, pp. 36–74.
13. Lazarus, A. "Behavior rehearsal vs. non-directive therapy vs. advice in effecting behavior change," *Behavior Research and Therapy, 4*, 1966, pp. 209–212.
14. Malan, D. *A Study of Brief Psychotherapy*. London: Tavistock Publications, 1963.
15. Menninger, K. *Theory of Psychoanalytic Techniques*. New York: Basic Books, 1958, pp. 15–42.
16. Phillips, E. L., and Wiener, D. N. *Short-term Psychotherapy and Structured Behavior Change*. New York: McGraw-Hill, 1966.
17. Rusk, T. N. "Principles of Psychotherapy," unpublished manuscript, 1971.
18. Rusk, T. N. "Opportunity and Technique in Crisis Psychiatry," *Comprehensive Psychiatry*, Vol. 12, no. 3, May 1971, pp. 249–263.
19. Small, L. *The Briefer Psychotherapies*. New York: Bruner/Mazel, 1971.
20. Truax, C., and Mitchell, K. "Research on Certain Therapist Interpersonal Skills in Relation to Process and Outcome," in *Handbook of Psychotherapy and Behavior Change*. Bergin, A., and Garfield, S. (Eds.). New York: Wiley, 1971, pp. 299–344.
21. Wolberg, L. *The Technique of Psychotherapy*. New York: Grune & Stratton, 1967.
22. Wolpe, J., and Lazarus, A. *Behavior Therapy Techniques*. Oxford: Pergamon Press, 1966.